Class of '79

Class of '79

*The story of three fellow students
who risked their lives to
destroy apartheid*

Janice Warman

First published by Jacana Media (Pty) Ltd in 2014

10 Orange Street
Sunnyside
Auckland Park 2092
South Africa
+2711 628 3200
www.jacana.co.za

ISBN 978-1-4314-1086-6

Cover photograph: Class of '79 Rhodes University, photograph courtesy
Marion Sparg collection
Cover design by publicide
Set in Sabon 10.75/15pt
Job no. 002220
Printed and bound by CTP Printers, Cape Town

ISO 12647 compliant

The author and publisher would like to acknowledge with thanks the
permission granted by the *Philadelphia Inquirer*.

See a complete list of Jacana titles at www.jacana.co.za

For all those who suffered under apartheid,
and suffered to end it.
And in particular, to Marion, Zubeida and Guy
for sharing their story.

The Baize Door

Faded green, rubbed, velvety, warm,
On one side, the new wall-to-wall;
On the other, the linoleum was worn.
At the jingling of the brass bell,
With a thwack of the flapping door,
Out came Beauty, forehead damp,
Apron skew, oval platter high with food.
We sat, majestical children, swathed
In linen. Our backs were straight.
We did not clear. We did not make beds.
We did not know where the soap was kept,
Or the clean sheets. The pool sparkled.
The trees did not shed their leaves.

– JANICE WARMAN

The child is not dead

The child is not dead
The child lifts his fists against his mother
Who shouts Afrika! shouts the breath
Of freedom and the veld
In the locations of the cordoned heart

The child lifts his fists against his father
in the march of the generations
who shouts Afrika! shout the breath
of righteousness and blood
in the streets of his embattled pride

The child is not dead not at Langa nor at Nyanga
not at Orlando nor at Sharpeville
nor at the police station at Philippi
where he lies with a bullet through his brain

The child is the dark shadow of the soldiers
on guard with rifles Saracens and batons
the child is present at all assemblies and law-givings
the child peers through the windows of houses and
into the hearts of mothers
this child who just wanted to play in the sun at Nyanga is
everywhere
the child grown to a man treks through all Africa

The child grown into a giant journeys through the whole world
Without a pass

– INGRID JONKER, MARCH 1960

Contents

The Beginning

WHEN DID THIS BOOK BEGIN? It's hard to say. This is one version of the answer: I was back in South Africa for the election in 2009, writing a couple of pieces for *The Spectator* magazine. I had been thinking for years about writing the extraordinary story of three fellow journalism students at Rhodes University, who, thirty years before, had risked their lives to fight apartheid, and this seemed to be the moment. I proposed the idea to *The Observer* editor John Mulholland, and the magazine carried a feature.

But really it had begun ten years earlier, in 1999, when I opened my new copy of Antjie Krog's *Country of My Skull,* her excoriating, illuminating, incandescent tale of South Africa's Truth and Reconciliation Commission. The book fell open in my hands to the page containing this quote and I was transfixed: *And the next thing he came back and he beat me right across the room into the wall and he kept on beating me right into the wall and I felt myself going down.* It was Zubeida's evidence to the commission, delivered, I imagined, in a brave, clear voice suffused with the pain I was to hear a decade later: *... a man came in, and he said to the man, 'Just rape her, just rape her...'.*[1] As it turned out, they didn't rape her, but they did poison her. She escaped death, but only narrowly.

No, that too is wrong. It really began twenty years before that, when we were writing our subediting exam in our final year at Rhodes University, and we were called out in the middle of it to have our class photograph taken – the Class of '79. We milled about on the little slope by the exam hall and were called into rows. I was in the back row, Marion was in the middle and Zubeida refused to take part. 'It would only be used for propaganda purposes,' she pointed out with one of her dazzling, trademark smiles.

Within six months of that day, Marion had bombed the offices of the opposition Progressive Federal Party and left the country to join Umkhonto we Sizwe (The Spear of the Nation), the military wing of the African National Congress (ANC); Zubeida had been arrested and was being tortured for her exposé of apartheid evil in the *Cape Times*; and Guy Berger, betrayed by the spy Craig Williamson, had been arrested for possession of banned books. After seven months in custody, three of which he spent in solitary confinement, he was sentenced to four years in prison.

Yet, of course, it began far earlier for all three students. It began at the moment that each of them realised that what was happening in South Africa – the so-called separate development – was wrong, and that they simply couldn't tolerate it. And for all of them, that moment came at Rhodes University.

Each had a distinctive background, each grew up in a different part of the country: one in East London in the Eastern Cape, born to a German-Irish family; one in the close-knit Muslim community of Cape Town; and one on a smallholding outside Johannesburg, born to a Lithuanian father and an Australian mother. Even when they met, they did not immediately become friends, though certainly Marion and Zubeida admired Guy, who was a year ahead of us. Both women confided to me later that had they known how involved he was in politics already, they would have plunged in headlong right then.

Most white South Africans had grown up in the suburbs, in the sunshine and the luxury, unthinkingly accepting, as children do, the status quo. We were spoiled. Thoughtless. We had tea brought to us in bed in the morning; we did not need to tidy up after ourselves, ever. Our mothers wrote menus – other people shopped and cooked – and we sat, we ate, we did not clear. So despite this luxury – different degrees of it, of course; we didn't all have mothers who wrote menus – what turned some of us into revolutionaries?

Some of us grew up in highly politicised families. Guy and Marion did not; Zubeida's family was the most politically aware. Yet, each of them chose to reject their backgrounds and take the path of resistance, following in the footsteps of the famous few. Among these were the writers: Breyten Breytenbach, Nadine Gordimer, Ingrid Jonker, Alan Paton. And the fighters: Albie Sachs, Ruth First, Trevor Manuel, Joe Slovo.

And apart from these rightly celebrated figures, there are others, less well known, who simply did what they thought was right. Many died. Neil Aggett was the first white activist to die in detention at the hands of the security police, and to their astonishment, his death sparked an international outcry.

Then there were the exiles who were murdered, victims of the overseas operations of the white government. There were many, including Ruth First, killed by a parcel bomb; Jeannette Schoon, blown up with her daughter Katryn, in place of her husband Marius, the intended target; and Albie Sachs, who lost an arm but survived. These three were the victims of Craig Williamson, the self-styled, and seemingly remorseless, 'superspy'. It was Williamson who was responsible for the first arrest of Guy Berger and who pitched up during his second detention, fresh from Moscow and so arrogant that Guy soon realised that he was there to justify himself and boast of his achievements rather than to conduct an interrogation.

But it wasn't even necessary to be politically involved in order to attract attention from the security police. When I was studying at Rhodes, I had strong views, but, like many opinionated students, I wasn't politically active. Imagine my shock when my brother-in-law Herman told me last year that my boyfriend (now husband) Julian and I had been under surveillance. Herman had gone to a wedding in the Boland. There he met twin sisters running a B&B whose family were friends of his parents in Blouberg, the holiday resort just outside Cape Town where they had a house. One of the twins had been in the security police, who had, they said, been following us at Rhodes, where, the police claimed, Julian had given a very large donation to the ANC. (He hadn't.) They went to see his Afrikaans mother at Blouberg. She persuaded them it wasn't Julian; together they decided the donation must have come from his English girlfriend – me. (It didn't.) It's a story that perhaps serves only to show that while the security police could be deadly effective much of the time, some of the time they had no idea what they were doing.

Then, of course, there was the other side. My friend Graham Watts, first my journalism lecturer at Rhodes and later a colleague at the *Financial Times,* told me over supper recently that he had been asked by the ANC to report on South Africans in the UK. They needed to know who were likely to be spies – journalists in particular. 'I can't remember if I had to report on you,' he said, a smile curving his lips. Later, I rang him, home by then in Bangkok. 'Did you?' I asked. 'Yes, I had to report on everybody.

In any event, there we were all those years ago, arriving at university fresh-faced and clear-eyed. 'For heaven's sake,' my father said, seeing me off at the airport, 'don't get drunk, don't get pregnant – and don't get involved in politics.'

He was right to be concerned. Rhodes University in the late seventies, with its Sir Herbert Baker-designed campus and its lush green lawns, looked prosperous and sedate. But the Sunday papers had been full of the escapades of its notorious drinking-club patrons and their loose morals; the Eastern Cape was, after the unrest of 1976, a place of turmoil and desperate poverty, and the campus was thought by most conservative parents to be a hotbed of political activity.

Nearby, the Nationalist Party government's policy of forced removals meant thousands of black people had been moved from the cities into the black 'homelands' of Transkei and Ciskei, where they were dumped with only a standpipe and a couple of huts for company.

Many children died in these homelands before the age of three from malnutrition. For the most part, their parents were unemployed and desperately poor.

We arrived in 1977, the year after the Soweto uprising, to enrol for the journalism degree. Months later, Steve Biko was murdered in custody. The campus tipped over into turmoil. There were demonstrations, meetings and hunger strikes.

So far, so ordinary for South Africa at the time. But for most of us, Rhodes was a revelation. We had been brought up to respect authority. Here, we were able to forge a whole new identity, personally and politically.

Out of that class of 1979 came two women whose identities merged with the painful birth of the new South Africa: two journalism students whose journey was to take them through defiance, imprisonment and torture during the apartheid years. One of the quietest girls in the class, Marion Sparg, joined Umkhonto we Sizwe, trained in exile in Angola and was eventually convicted of bombing two police stations. The *Cape Times* journalist Zubeida Jaffer was imprisoned and tortured for her writing and her union activism, yet ultimately chose not to prosecute her torturer.

Was there something special about the atmosphere of that journalism class at Rhodes? Today you can trace the footprints of my classmates across the opposition press in South Africa and, the liberal press in the UK – *The Guardian, The Observer* and, perhaps particularly, the *Financial Times* (*FT*). When I first worked at the *FT* in the late eighties, a rather peevish note was posted on the newsroom noticeboard. It read: *So you're a South African political refugee? And you want to be a journalist? Just take a cab from Heathrow to the FT. They'll look after you.*

For its students, me among them, Rhodes was a window on the outside world. For the first time we could engage in open political debate (although many of the books we wanted to read were banned by the government).

It was the home of the most highly regarded English department in the country, headed by the country's best-known white poet, Guy Butler, and home to the novelist André Brink (I remember queuing behind him on a Sunday morning at Paula's Bakery, famous for its sticky Chelsea buns). Because journalism was not a degree offered at 'black' universities, we had a scattering of black students in our class: this was certainly the first time many of us would ever have met anyone who was black who was not also a servant.

I went to hear a talk by Pik Botha, the foreign minister, now rehabilitated but then a Hitlerian figure with a narrow moustache, an imposing bulk and a posse of security men in royal-blue suits. His reception was suitably stormy, even mocking – students flapping their arms and chanting 'Pik-pik-pik-pik-P-I-I-I-K!' like chattering hens – but all students who asked a question had to identify themselves first. Guy Berger remembers standing up at the meeting and challenging Botha, pointing out that if the government banned critics from speaking, why should Rhodes provide the censors with a platform?

To the north, Angola was becoming the South African government's very own Vietnam, the site of a secret border war whose soldiers, mostly hapless conscripts on national service, came home paraplegic, traumatised or both. And in what was then Rhodesia, the war of independence was raging between Ian Smith and the rebel leaders, Robert Mugabe and Joshua Nkomo.

Our class was a strange mix of the naive, the frankly oblivious, the very political, and those who grew their own pot (*dagga*) and dried it on the washing line. If, on a Monday morning, half of us weren't in class, it was because we had either been caught smoking *dagga* or were in police detention. There were spies in every class. We never worked out who they were, although some of us suspected the friendly Afrikaans guy with the shark's-tooth necklace.

We studied the works of the Italian Communist Antonio Gramsci, who died in Mussolini's prisons, and Marshall McLuhan's writings about the global village. We learned about 'New Journalism', reading Joan Didion's *The White Album*, Tom Wolfe's *Electric Kool-Aid Acid Test* and Truman Capote's *In Cold Blood*. We drank tea on the lawn, went to Kenton-on-Sea for the weekend, and never made our beds or did our own laundry.

Les Switzer was our acting head of department during those years, when Prof Tony Giffard was overseas in the US. Switzer was one of those who went to court to give evidence for Guy; he knew all three activists as students. I tracked him down to Houston, Texas, where he is executive director of the Foundation for Contemporary Theology. As an American, the time spent in South Africa was life-changing for him:

Although I was regarded by some other academics as a leader of the 'neo-Marxist' school at Rhodes, my own view of what I was trying to do is somewhat different. My approach to teaching students in the world of the academy was to help prepare them for life by tutoring them to think in new ways about themselves and everything around them.

I wanted the students to embark on a process of interrogation that began with themselves, their upbringing and the society of which they were a part. In other words, I wanted them to begin by questioning their own assumptions – the presumptions we have about ourselves as women and men, the ways in which our lives are conditioned by circumstances beyond our control and the impact this has on how we see the world around us – beginning with who we are and how we view the 'other' we interact with on a daily basis.

The materialist paradigm was the starting point for me in this quest in the 1970s and 1980s. I saw it as an intellectually challenging approach for students in South Africa. We began with the classical Marxist ideas – class, capitalism and state – but soon moved into how power is exercised over the powerless in the modern capitalist state – mitigated by categories like gender and sexual orientation, colour and ethnic origin, occupation and income, and most significantly by language and ideology in a hegemonic 'democratic' culture. So you may remember reading articles, book chapters and essays by Ralph Miliband, Nicos Poulantzas, Antonio Gramsci, and in particular French and British cultural theorists like Louis Althusser, Raymond Williams and Stuart Hall.

But this wasn't simply an academic exercise. We also began reaching out to the community. Rhodes journalism department also played a small role in the larger picture with student newspapers like *Inquiry* that chronicled local struggles (mainly the 1980 'uprising' which we covered before, during and after it occurred); with participation in an alternative, local township newspaper called *Ilizwi LaseRhini/Grahamstown Voice* (mainly in Xhosa), a collaborative effort between Rhodes University students (including journalism students) and local African township residents. In journalism/writing workshops, some of us initiated with unregistered (i.e. illegal) trade unions, the Southern African Bishops Conference (then under the leadership of a priest who became a prominent figure in the ANC after 1994) and other anti-apartheid religious and secular groups.

By the time we left Rhodes, Donald Woods, a friend of Steve Biko and banned maverick newspaper editor of the *Daily Dispatch*, had successfully fled the country disguised as a priest. The government had banned so many people, organisations and newspapers that there was little left of what passed for an opposition.

Many of us, me among them, were planning to leave South Africa, neither happy to stay and enjoy a lifestyle based on the violent disenfranchisement of others, nor brave enough to stand up and fight.

A few of us were different. This is their story. I offer it with the greatest respect.

Johannesburg

AS THE PLANE TOUCHED DOWN at Johannesburg's OR Tambo airport, I was relaxed; I had even slept on the flight. I met my cousin Rory in the new World Cup-smart arrivals hall and we tried, unsuccessfully, to buy me a phone – in my rush to leave the UK, I'd left my South African cellphone behind. Then we went to get some money at an ATM after fending off a request for a handout from a white Zimbabwean who told us he had been living in the airport for a month. 'Always just say you don't carry cash,' Rory advised.

We set off for his car, balancing my suitcases and camera case on the trolley. And then it began. It's hard to say exactly where the man materialised from, but suddenly he was there, chatting, helping Rory pay for the parking at the machine, then pushing the trolley. He was smartly dressed, very at ease. Most important of all, my cousin, who had lived in Joburg all his life, seemed quite relaxed. I wasn't worried, but I did ensure I carried my own handbag and camera case.

When we got to the car, Rory began loading the cases into the boot. With his head under the lid, he was out of sight. The man opened the back door of the car and turned to take my camera case. Out of sheer politeness, I gave it to him – I didn't want him to think I didn't trust him. Then he put his hands on my handbag, which was slung over my arm – I was holding a bottle of water in that hand, which provided a natural stop to what he was trying to do. I resisted slightly – there was no need, I was going to be sitting in the front of the car. But he tugged at it, saying nothing. And I gave it to him! The same impulse that had driven my decision to give him the camera case, with several thousand rands' worth of Canon equipment in it, prompted me to remove the bottle from my hand and hand the bag – with everything important in it, from passport to driver's licence, jewellery and, of course, my purse – to a complete stranger. He rewarded my trust: he put it in the car.

Then my cousin reappeared. He gave the man a tip and we got in the car. I idly noticed that he had disappeared, leaving the trolley swivelling slightly in his wake. 'He should have taken it,' Rory remarked.

We discussed him no further. We had so much to talk about, as I hadn't seen Rory for decades. Later, of course, I recalled how odd it all was – there are uniformed staff to help with trolleys, precisely because of persistent problems with con men. We hadn't needed any help with the trolley. And my cousin, not our self-appointed guide, had loaded the cases into the boot.

Because, of course, the suitcases were of no interest to our friend. Even the cameras weren't of any interest, nor were the credit cards, the passport, the driver's licence, the small bag of earrings in my handbag – none of it. What was of interest was my purse, in which I had just neatly stowed the equivalent of about R5 000 – an absolute fortune to the man and his family.

It all seemed so obvious – later. Afterwards, when I was unpacking in my Sandton B&B, my angel of a proprietress offered to drive me into town to get the local cellphone I had failed to buy at the airport. I dug around in my bag. No purse. It had to be there. Eventually, I upended the bag on the bed. I looked under the bed. I rang my cousin, convinced I must have dropped it in his car. I simply couldn't believe it. Of course, now I realised what had happened. As he took my bag, the man had briefly turned his back to me and neatly stowed it beside the camera case. In doing so, I now belatedly reckoned, he had partially unzipped it and levered out the purse. No wonder he had shot off so fast.

I had been watched, I was told. Someone had seen me arrive at the airport and observed me bumbling around looking for a cellphone, and then – big, big mistake – getting some cash out of an ATM. All absolute rookie mistakes from a soft European newly arriving at a developing-world airport – even one that looked far smarter than Heathrow. The irony was that I had just come back from Nairobi: I wouldn't have dreamed of doing it there.

I was lucky, of course. I was told that if I had resisted, the man would simply have cut the bag off my arm and I may well have been injured in the process. So perhaps my politeness saved me.

I rang my bank. 'We can't send your debit card to South Africa,' I was told. 'Why not?' I asked. 'It's a dangerous country' was the response.' 'I know,' I said. 'I've just been robbed.'

The owner of my B&B kindly took me to the police station to report the theft. When I was giving my statement, the policewoman told me that one day she had been happily walking along a busy street, only to realise eventually that someone had deftly made a long cut in her bag, everything had fallen out, and the thief had simply picked up what he wanted and scarpered. She laughed. 'I had my car stolen three years ago from where I parked it one day,' she continued. 'Today all my colleagues were laughing at me because I finally reported it missing. I know there is no point – it will never be found.'

Well, that was my introduction to Joburg. And like many white South Africans, I became obsessed with my experience, forgetting instantly that the vast majority of crimes – robberies, rapes, murders – do not happen to privileged whites, and, in particular, not to those who are only dipping into the country for a story.

I learned a lot in those first few days. My B&B owner let me ring the UK in search of reissued credit cards and money transfers. I had to use a phone attached to her fax-machine line as she had just had several thousand rands' worth of telephone calls stolen by people who had camped outside the high boundary walls and the barbed wire and the burglar alarms. Thankfully the telephone company let her off. After all, it was happening all over Joburg – and with electrical wiring and copper plumbing too.

Her husband drove me through Parkhurst to see the massive mansions he had built in a former life. The walls were high and the security gates massive. In one concreted entrance there was a guard suspended, in a glass-walled office about twenty feet up a tower. 'I suppose that's a development of several houses,' I ventured naively. 'Oh no,' he said. 'That's just one person's home.'

I had deliberately made my Joburg visit short. Aside from my old friend Rob Harrewyn and a former colleague from the *Financial Times*, Peter Bruce,[2] now editor of *Business Day*, I didn't have any friends to see. I had only one person to interview, and frankly, I was nervous.

I was there to see Marion Sparg. She was one of my subjects: she had been the quiet girl at the back of the class who said little, who got high marks, who joined nothing. Yet after university, she and two colleagues had bombed the offices of the white liberal Progressive Federal Party (PFP).[3] Then she had left to train with Umkhonto we Sizwe (MK), the military wing of the ANC, one of the very few white women to do so.

I was to see her on Saturday at her home with her children; I was flying out on Sunday. As much as I looked forward to our meeting, all my feelings of insecurity about the book flooded through me. Who was I to write it? The three people who were my subjects had fought the system, been tortured, imprisoned. They hadn't run away – I had. While I had been reporting on flower shows in the UK, Marion had been marching in the dust of Botswana and Zubeida had defied the torturers who had poisoned her. While I had ridden my horse across the Sussex Downs, Guy had deliberately pleaded guilty in order to release his friends from being forced to bear state witness against him or go to prison themselves, thus condemning himself to prison. Later, while Zubeida was rearrested and tortured again, I was at the BBC, the *FT* and the *Guardian*, reporting on the Big Bang, Black Monday, the stock market crash, city scandals; it was all a world away.

Yes, who was I to write their story? How dare I? Then it was Saturday, and as I sat in Marion's house, one of the things she said to me was the following: 'I remember this one young junior advocate who came in to help me, and he said he felt it was necessary for him to explain to me why he hadn't got involved in the struggle.' She laughed as she recalled, 'I said to him, "But why do you think you need to justify anything to me, for heaven's sake?" '

I explained to her that that was just how I felt, as a father might if a child had said in the 1950s, 'What did you do in the war, Daddy?' and that this was why I wanted to write this book. I had the feeling that she understood, because she told me what she told the young man: 'I suppose why I found it strange was that people were contributing in very many different ways. I was aware that there was a whole defence team that was defending me; they were playing a very vital role.'

So we went on talking, and she took me step by step through her story: her motivations, her actions and her exile; her training; and her re-entries into South Africa, always on foot with a rucksack, when the police would stop and lecture her on the dangers of hitchhiking and give her a lift to the nearest town. And then, of course, the placing of the limpet mines, the waiting, the living alone, and then the betrayal and the arrests. And the solitary confinement, the interrogation, the trial and the imprisonment.

So this was how it went: the taxi ride to her house through the streets strewn with jacaranda blossoms, and through areas where I certainly wouldn't want to walk alone, lively with shops and people. I felt foreign here, separated by a gap that thirty years had created. I felt I was reaching through the dark for the truth. But this was something I wanted to do, and I wanted to do it well.

PART ONE

Marion Sparg

HILLBROW, JOHANNESBURG. 7 March 1986. Marion was bent over the bath in her flat, washing clothes, pondering her next move. She had just returned from a trip to the shops. She had been followed; she knew that. Normally – and this was normal in her world – you would be followed for days or weeks, sometimes even months.

So, then, she had time to move. She could disappear back over the border as quickly as she had come: a white girl with a rucksack.

Only this time it would be lighter. Because the limpet mines were gone.

Then it came. A knock; no one had ever knocked at her door before.

She approached cautiously and pulled the blue curtain across its wire rods. A woman stood there. She was nervous; she looked to her side.

Now Marion knew what was coming. She backed slowly away from the door.

Then, as what followed began to happen, seemingly in slow motion, she was back in Maseru with her commander.

I want a gun for this job. I want a gun.

No. I will not give you a gun. If I give you one, you'll use it. And if you use it, you'll end up dead.

I want a gun.

There will be more of them than you. And if you use the gun,

1

they'll kill you. You might kill one of them, but they will kill you. Marion, trust me here. You can't take a gun.

Now there were at least five policemen in the room and she was on the floor. She hadn't opened the door; it was hanging off its hinges. And they were shouting, jostling her, screaming obscenities.

And then she was angry. Not afraid – angry.

'I was furious,' Marion tells me. 'Furious because there was nothing I could do. There were security policemen all over me with two pistols on either side of my head. A dangerous situation. A situation in which it is best to remain calm if you want to come out alive. But I was too angry and so the shouting match continued. And then I remember the lieutenant in charge, who had remained outside, walked in and said, "Stop shouting, everybody!" '

She laughs. 'It was a bit crazy. But that anger was so real and so unexpected. It came from nowhere.

'I had now been handcuffed and seated on the bed. The lieutenant who had come in and calmed the situation down sat down next to me. He gave me some piece of paper where he was described as an officer of the peace.

'I saw these words and lost it again. I screamed at him. I remember this poor guy looking at me like he was thinking, Have I met a lunatic here? And he said, "What has made you so angry?" And I said, "How can you describe yourself as an officer of the *peace*?"'

It was a situation that Marion would meet again and again: the sheer farcical nature of exchanges with the law. South Africa under apartheid had an Orwellian air. There may not have been a Ministry of Truth, but the 'Ministry of Co-operation and Development' ran the apartheid system, which was itself called 'separate development'. Then there was the 'Ministry of Justice' – applying laws that countered human rights. The 'Immorality Act' that rendered any sex act across the racial divide an imprisoning offence saw many police officers spying on couples through keyholes before rushing in to make an arrest.

Marion was kept in the flat for several hours while the police completed their search. Then she was brought before a magistrate to make a statement saying she had not been assaulted during her arrest. Finally, that night she was taken back to one of her bomb targets of three days before: John Vorster Square, the police station that was infamous for detentions and interrogations. Unlike most political detainees, Marion was both white and a woman. 'I could see throughout the whole time they really were not sure how to keep me or deal with me at all,' she says.

Her interrogating officer had also questioned Guy Berger. (And back in 1977, when he was head of the Security Branch in Grahamstown, the officer had also arrested Steve Biko, the Black Consciousness Movement leader who would die in detention.) 'During my interrogation, he would often refer to Guy, almost with a kind of respect,' Marion recalls. 'Brigadier Alfred Oosthuizen was his name. He would say, "Guy Berger, now *he* really knew what he was doing." He was fixated on white people who were in the ANC, because if he wasn't talking about Guy, he would be talking about Ronnie Kasrils[4] or Joe Slovo.[5] In the heads of the security police, it was white people who were running the ANC. They just couldn't believe that blacks were capable of doing anything. He was strangely obsessed with Joe Slovo. He saw him as evil personified – but at the same time, there was a reluctant tone of admiration in his voice when he spoke about Joe.

'Oosthuizen was a nasty character, not pleasant at all. A colleague I work with today often uses a term that describes him so well: *glibberige jakkals*.[6] After my release, there were some comrades who said Oosthuizen wanted to have a discussion with me. And I said, "He's the last man I ever want to see again." Not that he did anything worse than what anyone else did. But he struck me as someone with serious issues and I wanted nothing to do with him.'

There was another factor. The Olivia Forsyth story had been all over the papers. She was a British-born spy who had infiltrated activist groups at Rhodes University and then the University of Cape Town in the early

1980s. Later, as a lieutenant in the security police, she infiltrated the ANC. She was eventually exposed, held (and tortured) in the infamous Quatro camp in Angola for four years before escaping to the UK.

Oosthuizen would later manage Forsyth, and it would strike Marion that many of the questions he posed to her were almost as if he was trying to solve Forsyth issues by testing Marion's knowledge and experience of the ANC.

'The whole story came out while I was in prison,' she says. 'I remember reading that he was the security policeman who was working with Olivia. It all suddenly made sense. He knew that there was no way I was going to agree to work with him. He was trying to use me to solve problems for Olivia Forsyth, painting scenarios: "So what if you were to agree to work with us and we released you and you went back to Lusaka?"[7] And I said, "How could I just be released and go back to Lusaka?" And he would say, "We would arrange an escape," and I said, "Yes, and when you arrange an escape it would be a very convenient way of just shooting someone in the back, saying they were killed trying to escape."

'I said to him, "What would possibly motivate me to work for you? What could possibly motivate me?" And he said, "Money." And I said, "If I agree I'm going back to Lusaka, what am I going to do with money in Lusaka? I'm going to be living as an ANC comrade. You don't go shopping when you are in exile in places like Lusaka and in the camps in Angola, so exactly how am I going to enjoy this money that you are going to offer me?" '

Marion is laughing as she recounts the story. We are sitting in the cool of her terracotta dining room in Observatory, Joburg, with her children at one end of the big table doing their maths homework, the purple jacaranda blossoms lying thick on the lawn, and the brown Burmese cat Ruby contributing the occasional guttural yowl. Michelle (age eleven) brings us tea; Joy (six) decides to serenade us with a Disney number, but is persuaded that it may interfere with the tape recording. The cat dramatically gets her neck caught in the string of the blind and has to be rescued. The symbolism is lost on the children, but in all likelihood, not on Marion.

What astounds me is the amount of merriment that punctuates her story. Did she laugh at the time, I ask her, or did the sheer ridiculousness of some of the events only strike her with the benefit of distance?

'There were certainly times it was funny. Obviously it was not all fun and games. There were dark times and desperate times. But the police did make me laugh. I had thought they were going to be so clever, and yet ... I remember Oosthuizen didn't like it. He used to get really angry at times, because he would tell me that I was humouring him. I would say, "What else must I do but humour you?"'

'They weren't gentle, but I was never physically tortured in any way. There was rough handling, *ja*, but nothing that I didn't expect. But I don't want to give the impression that it was easy. At the end of the day, your life was in their hands.

'There were very dark days and terrible times in John Vorster Square. Times where you were simply desperate to be with those you left behind in exile.

'It was the people I had kept inside my head and heart from exile that kept me going at times like these. I used to have long conversations in my head with Thabo [Mbeki], Chris [Hani], Janet [Love] and Joe [Slovo]. At times, when I did not know how to react to a situation, the first thing that would pop into my head was, What would Thabo do about this? How would Janet have responded to this?

'When I was just too lonely, I would write letters in my head to these and other individuals. I wish I could remember some of those letters now. All gone with time, sadly. But they kept me busy and focused on something other than those four grey walls.

'Oosthuizen and his team knew I was going to end up on trial. So they were very careful about not wanting to go through another Neil Aggett ordeal. And I could also sense the fact that I was a white woman influenced the way they treated me. I was a terrorist, yes, but a white woman first. Crazy, but true.'

Twenty-eight-year-old Dr Neil Aggett, a trade union organiser with the Food and Canning Workers' Union who had organised several successful strikes, had died in John Vorster Square in 1982, allegedly by his own hand – the first white South African activist to die in custody. After a six-month inquest, opinion was divided as to whether he had hanged himself as a result of brutal and prolonged torture or whether he had died as a result of the torture itself, which had included electric shocks, prolonged assaults and days of non-stop interrogation.

The subsequent outcry, both in South Africa and abroad, meant that the security police did not want another white prisoner dying in custody, if they could help it. Aggett's funeral was attended by 15 000 people – and as Bishop Desmond Tutu pointed out at the time, this activist was a white man who was mourned almost exclusively by black people.

The world in which Marion was arrested was only four years away from the release of Nelson Mandela in 1990, but it may as well have been decades. There had been not one but two States of Emergency declared, in 1985 and 1986. Her two fellow students from Rhodes, Guy Berger and Zubeida Jaffer, had been arrested, detained, interrogated, imprisoned (in Guy's case) and tortured (in Zubeida's case), but released. Mandela's release had been predicted, then denied; Neil Aggett's detention and death had flashed around the world. And then, just as they had done in 1980, the prison gates had clanged shut once more on the prospect of liberation.

All of these things had an effect on Marion's own detention. Being kept in solitary confinement for three months gave her the opportunity to think back to how it had all started.

* * *

She had grown up in the Eastern Cape in a 'typical white, middle-class, South African, English-speaking' family with a German-Irish background. She was one of six children.

'My family were not political. I matriculated in 1976, and one teacher did have an impact on me. Ironically, it was our Afrikaans teacher, Jack Visser, who came into the class on 16 June 1976 and asked us if we knew what was happening in Soweto.[8] He was disgusted when he realised what an uninformed lot we were. He was not your typical Afrikaans teacher. He knew my love of poetry and introduced me to the work of Ingrid Jonker,[9] and he would call me into his office and talk about Afrikaans literature.

However, she adds, 'Rhodes was really where the politicisation began, and most of it was a response to Steve Biko's murder at the hands of the security police. It was not just the circumstances of his death that were shocking, but the reaction on Rhodes campus that really shocked me – the complete lack of concern from most students and the outright glee from many others. Most of them did not even know who Steve was and what he stood for before his death. He was just "another terr [terrorist]" and his death was something to celebrate as far as they were concerned.

'I was also deeply moved by the manner in which Donald Woods [Biko's friend and editor of the *Daily Dispatch*, the liberal East London newspaper] handled the death and what he published in the *Dispatch* at that time. His response was so at odds with what I was experiencing on campus.'

After university, Marion joined fellow journalists in a one-day sympathy strike at the *Sunday Times* in 1981 in a show of solidarity for black journalists who were on strike. 'We were told that we had avoided dismissal "by the skin of our teeth". These were the so-called liberal editors who told us that the only reason they had not dismissed us was because they would then also have had to fire all the black journalists on strike. After that, I gave up on journalists being able to achieve anything meaningful.'

Soon after joining the *Sunday Times*, she and two colleagues bombed the offices of the opposition PFP when it refused to join a planned anti-Republic Day[10] protest – 'a rather clumsy and ill-considered action, I realise with hindsight,' she says with understatement. (It was, in fact, the only thing for which she was later to apologise in court.)

Shortly after these events, she and journalist-activist Damian de Lange were contacted by the renowned cleric and legendary Afrikaner anti-apartheid campaigner Beyers Naudé, who told them they had to leave the country as they were about to be arrested. It all happened very fast. 'I don't think either of us knew much about the ANC either, and we certainly weren't aware of the extent of it at all in exile,' Marion says.

(Damian, who was also imprisoned in 1986, was released, like Marion, in 1991, and became a brigadier general in the South African Navy and Defence Force before launching a military equipment company selling military vehicles and goods internationally. He lives close to Marion, in nearby Kensington.)

So their departure was arranged. 'Comrades in exile at the time had the idea that if you were white, you got on a plane and flew to the ANC in London. Instead, some guys drove Damian and me to what was then the Bophuthatswana[11] border. It was some time after midnight and we walked across. The guys walked across with us and pointed us in the general direction. We knew more or less what part of the border we were crossing, so we had some idea of what towns to head for.'

What were you carrying with you?

'Just knapsacks, with a few things. The area was totally deserted – this was near Mafikeng, the border post. We walked for a couple of hours that night and then slept.'

So you just lay down on the ground and slept?

'Yes, and then the next morning we walked for another hour or two. There wasn't a lot of traffic but there was some. The area was mostly unoccupied, almost like wild desert. There were a couple of farms. And then we hitchhiked most of the way to Gaborone [the capital of Botswana]. We had been given contacts to get hold of and eventually the people we were put in touch with were Jeannette and Marius Schoon, and we stayed with them for a couple of days.

'Then they put us in touch with the person I later worked with in the Scorpions, or Directorate of Special Operations, in 2000: Pete Richer.[12] It was early June then, and Diana Cumberledge – Damian's partner at the time – joined us. She was pregnant with twins. Just after she arrived, the twins were born. I left shortly after that, not knowing if I would ever see them again, and went through to Lusaka.

'I had decided I wanted to be part of the armed struggle and so from Lusaka I went for military training in Angola.

'I didn't really know what to expect. Luanda was very much a military town. There were lots of soldiers around – the Soviets, Cubans and the Angolans themselves, of course.' Marion was expecting to arrive at a military camp, but Caxito looked like a smallholding out in the bush.

'There were never more than 100 to 150 people there. There was a house that was being used as the command centre, and it was on a slight rise so you looked down over a valley, where the camp was, but when you stood there you could see nothing, just some trees, just like a valley. You thought, Where is the camp? We're in the middle of the bush. And then someone pointed out, "There's a tent here and there" – so it didn't look like the traditional military camp at all.'

Marion was one of only three women at Caxito. Another was Geraldine, now Geraldine Fraser-Moleketi, who served as minister of public service under former President Thabo Mbeki. 'Geraldine only stayed for a couple of weeks,' Marion recalls. 'She was on her way out as she had finished her training. There was one other woman, called Tsidi. I didn't know her surname, but it wouldn't have been her real name. She had also finished her training.

'So for most of the time I was the only woman there and also the only white person. Caxito was a bit different in the sense that you were either going there for undercover-type training, like myself and Geraldine, or there were people that the ANC didn't really want to expose to the bigger crowd of people in the camps where you had thousands of people.'

In fact, so unusual a sight was a white woman that when Joe Slovo, the veteran anti-apartheid campaigner and husband of the activist Ruth First, visited the camp, he presumed she was one of the female Soviet commanders. Told she was South African, he had her called to the command centre up on the hill so he could have a closer look at her.

After that brief first encounter, Slovo was to become a father figure to Marion (and to her fellow exile Janet Love, whom she met in Lusaka). She also came to know other leading exiles, including [now President] Jacob Zuma, whom she remembers telling stories of his childhood to a rapt audience gathered around him.

'When I think about Zuma in exile days, the picture that springs to mind is of him sitting in a chair in a house in Lusaka, with a group of comrades sitting around his feet. He's a wonderful storyteller. His stories were funny and captivating. They were made more so because they were always a mixture of fact and fiction. A lot of them were about his boyhood growing up in rural KwaZulu-Natal. They always had some kind of lesson to teach.

'I suppose to some extent I was treated differently – with kid gloves at times. I was fortunate because I was trained in camps like Caxito and Pango, which were smaller. They were the camps where MK members went before being sent back into South Africa. There was, therefore, not such an emphasis on basic military training, marching and drilling, and all that stuff.

'Instead, the emphasis was on getting people ready to operate inside the country. The spirit at these camps was also very different because of the type of cadres that were there. The cadres in Caxito had discipline and morale, and were excited about going home to fight, although some did become despondent because it seemed it was taking too long. Things didn't always work out according to plan.

'They came to Caxito to get used to working as a unit, to train in specialist skills, and to try to acclimatise themselves to operating inside the country. They had done so much "march and drill" in the big camps, so the challenge now was to try to get them to stop walking like soldiers [she laughs] – to make them seem like they came from Soweto again.

'You also had a lot of commanders from the front visiting Caxito. They would come in and assess the guys to see if they were ready to come in, so in many ways I was really lucky to get to know some remarkable fighters and individuals.

'There's a flip side to that too, of course. I think, from that time I trained in Caxito, there are only a handful of those who were in camp with me at the time who are still alive today. Most of them ended up being killed, either inside the country or in the frontline states.'

How?

'Mostly shootouts, that type of thing.

'Another advantage of training in Caxito, because it was smaller, was that you got a lot more individual attention during the training compared to when you were part of thousands in the big camps.

'During the time I spent in Caxito and later in Pango, when I trained again in 1984, there were no more than two women in the camp (me being one of them), and at times I was the only woman in camp with a couple of hundred MK members. When I tell certain people this today, they look at me in horror and ask if I was afraid. A white woman all on her own in a camp with 100 trained black men? I can honestly say that I have never felt more at home, more safe than I did then.'

But being very often the only woman had its own challenges. 'Many comrades had not seen or interacted with women for a long time. So one had to get used to getting ten marriage proposals a day – and, more importantly, had to learn how to deal with these with the firmness and the sensitivity they required. Overall, in the camps I was in, women were treated well.

'I became aware later that other women did not fare so well in other camps. But I felt safe, protected and even nurtured.'

But the feminist spark did emerge now and then. 'I remember being outraged when a comrade brought me flowers on Women's Day. I was a soldier and resented being treated like a flower of the nation. But later, I realised what a mission it must have been to find flowers in the middle of the bush in Angola and had to apologise for being so rude.

11

He was the camp medic, a comrade called Bob, and was so proud of the bunch of flowers he had found, who knows where.

'The most wonderful thing that happened – and I realised this only much later – was that during the time I spent in Caxito back in 1982, I quite literally forgot that I was white. I know that will never happen in my life again.'

She trained for nine months in Caxito. 'I was lucky because the camp was small and a lot of it was individual training. There was either just me or one or two people with me, like when I did training in explosives or firearms. I was very lucky, because afterwards I heard that in the bigger camps, you were lucky if you got the opportunity to fire an AK once. It was all a lot more intensive and individualised in Caxito.

'I would do my firearms and explosives training alone with a trainer all to myself. It was only in political education classes that I joined bigger groups.'

Did you have full firearms training and full explosives training?

'Yes, the training included firearms, explosives, MCW or military and combat work, which taught you how to operate underground, fieldwork and topography, and, of course, political education.

'It was intensive. I would spend days out on the hills surrounding Caxito with my trainer blowing up TNT in all sorts of formations. We also spent a lot of time practising all the tricks the Vietnamese used against the Americans, shooting explosives into the air to take down helicopters, laying out minefields and so on, all sorts of booby traps. But that was really all for fun and to get used to handling explosives.

'We knew that it was limpet mines I would be using. But those were precious and you couldn't blow up too many of those. So we had to settle for TNT.

'I'm aware that I may be making this sound like it was all fun and games. We were aware of the dangers involved and took every precaution. The dangers were brought home when my trainer and I arrived back in camp one day, very hot and tired after hours in the bush, to find that another group training not far from us had met with tragedy. A landmine had gone off prematurely. To save the lives of those he was training, the trainer threw himself forward, losing his eyes and hands in the process.'

After nine months, Marion went back to Lusaka and was deployed to the ANC Women's League, working on *VOW* (*Voice of Women*) magazine. This required a lot of travel between Luanda and Lusaka. She was taking articles written in Lusaka through to the printing house in Luanda and returning with printed material to go to the forward areas. 'The purpose of the articles was to mobilise the population in South Africa; there wasn't really much news you could provide. We were either writing about individuals in the ANC or doing interviews with the ANC leaders, and we also were recording Radio Freedom in Lusaka, at the Zambian Broadcasting Services studio at that time.

'And then, in December 1982, that was when the first Maseru killings[13] had happened. It was after that that I started agitating to go back to South Africa. I said that I wanted to come back to the country, and it took a while, but towards the end of 1983, I came back to Angola for refresher training at a camp called Pango, which was further north than Caxito.

The war between the South African regime in alliance with Angolan rebels fighting the MPLA[14] government was still in full swing. In many ways it was South Africa's Vietnam – but unlike Vietnam, the first true media war, this was a secret war, strongly denied by the government. Soldiers who had been drafted into the army disappeared on assignment to fight the MPLA, the guerrilla organisation SWAPO[15] and their Cuban helpers came back with post-traumatic stress, dreadfully injured or not at all.

Marion was on the other side of that conflict. 'The Cubans were still in Angola at that time; I didn't train with them, but they were in the camps and they did a lot of training with some of the guys. They did the heavier training with the heavier guns and the rocket launchers.' The Soviets, she adds, were also doing some training with the heavier military equipment.

13

'You talk about the "secret war",' Marion says. 'If we needed any medical treatment, we used to go to the Cuban military hospitals. And it was shattering. I remember the first time I went, I needed to see the dentist. You'd sit and wait, and the ambulances didn't stop arriving, with young Cuban soldiers being flown in from the border with South West [Namibia] – it was shattering to see the number of injuries and young lives lost. I remember sitting and watching the stretchers pass and being aware that these young men were putting their lives on the line for my country.'

After Marion had moved north to Pango, shortly before Christmas 1983, news came that the South African Air Force was coming to bomb the camp. 'We had to move out and set up a temporary camp in the forest.'

The war in Angola hadn't reached fever pitch then; it began building up in earnest after Marion's departure. But there were battles between the South Africans and the combined Soviet/Cuban/Angolan force they were facing.

'There was a wonderful Soviet commander – I remember we just used to call him "George",' she recalls. 'He used to come and give us news of the frontline. He was quite a character. He carried more guns on his body than anyone I had ever seen, and the comrades used to tease him mercilessly about this. But he took it all in his stride.'

Marion was doing her refresher course at Pango, preparing to go back into the country for the first time since leaving in 1981. So often the only woman in camp, she was now one of three, and then two.

Then came New Year's Eve. Everyone had to take turns doing guard duty. 'There were some outposts really, really far from camp that we used to hate going to. On New Year's Eve, I had to go and sit at this outpost that I really hated. Pango was a jungle area, not the type of bushveld we were used to in many areas of Angola.

'I can remember sitting there on my own, remembering stories the comrades used to tease one another about – that there was a hyena that would frequent this particular post and you had to be careful. It had never bothered me before. But that night...

'There was an Angolan camp not too far away. And I remember at midnight hearing them celebrating and shooting and I was thinking, Here I am sitting alone in the bush and it's New Year's Eve. I longed for the guards commander to arrive. There were many guarding posts around the camp and a guards commander would patrol these every night, visiting each post in turn to check that everything was okay. His arrival was particularly welcome that night. Some human contact on such a dark night.'

And you would have been sitting there with what, just an AK-47?

'*Ja*, just an AK.'

Were you a good shot?

'Yes, I was, with an AK, not so much with the pistol. The first time I was given an AK to shoot in Caxito, my trainer looked at me and told me I was lying when I said I had never handled a gun before. I became quite indignant, but decided to take it as a compliment.

'Damian was also an excellent shot and later became a firearms trainer. He told me that the reason why women were better shots was because they were prepared to learn. Male comrades, he said, were always full of attitude and bravado and wouldn't listen. The best shots among the Soviets who trained in Caxito were also women. They agreed with Damian. The men's attitude was always, "You can't teach me, I know how to shoot".' She laughs.

And I have a vivid picture of Marion out in the bush in the dark, on her own, packing an AK-47; the pitch-dark and nothing but stars above; then the distant shots and laughter at midnight as the New Year of 1983 came in, a New Year that was less than a decade away from the shift of power she was fighting for.

Before going back to South Africa, Marion was working closely with Joe Slovo and Chris Hani,[16] who were in charge of the special operations division of MK. She did, however, have a strange introduction to Lesotho.

'Things do go wrong, although people don't like to talk about it. The first time I was sent through to Lesotho, I flew in with a false passport, and it didn't even occur to me until much later that the name they'd put into the passport was Mary Woods.' Marion later learned that Mary was the second name of Donald Woods's wife, Wendy. She had been told who to contact in Lesotho, but they just didn't materialise. No one answered her calls.

So she flew back to Lusaka and succeeded in talking her way out of the airport into the city, then contacted Chris Hani again. It turned out that there had been wild stories in the newspapers that Wendy Woods, who had gone into exile with Donald Woods, was back in Lesotho.

Marion flew back to Lesotho a few weeks later (Wendy Woods was in London with her husband by then), and this time she made contact with the people who had quite sensibly decided it might have been too dangerous to openly welcome 'Wendy Woods'.

Was there a warrant out for your arrest?

'I never found out if there was a warrant out, but there must have been.'

Once based in Maseru, Marion was travelling in and out of South Africa regularly, spending one to two months there at a time doing reconnaissance work, working out what were the appropriate targets and what was the best way to get to them. 'I wasn't attempting to set up a network, because it had been agreed that I would pretty much be working on my own with my commander in Lesotho, Eddie [Edward] Mabitsela.'

At that time the ANC had decided that 'soft targets' such as cinemas, shopping centres and restaurants were legitimate, but Marion told Eddie that she would be sticking to hard targets – police stations or military installations. He agreed.

'I would either get a lift across the border, or walk through the border and then just hitchhike. I didn't have a vehicle at any time, so I was literally hiking around the country. It sounds crazy when I say it now, but it worked. It was actually the South African police who gave me lifts in lots of places.'

The police would ask her what on earth she was doing travelling alone as a white woman. They would offer her a lift to the nearest station to put her on a train. 'I would say, "No, I can't sit on a train for three days, I'm just going to hike." I suppose I was lucky.' What Marion found most difficult when she came back into the country – 'quite simply being treated as a white South African' – was something Slovo had warned her about. And yet, it was the colour of her skin that enabled her to get into three police stations to place the bombs – in Johannesburg's notorious police headquarters, John Vorster Square; Cambridge police station in East London; and the Hillbrow police station.

Her colour was no protection against arrest, however. She was certainly betrayed by someone, but she never found out who it was. 'Who knows?' she says. 'It would appear that the security police definitely got information from someone about my being in the country and where to find me. Comrades have spoken to me about this and mentioned possible names and so on. But really, I did not come into the country expecting to survive for very long without being arrested.'

(In later years, other comrades told Marion who it was they thought had betrayed her. But she did not raise it with him, and now, after his death, she does not feel it would be fair to share her suspicions – a decision that bears out the great weight she gives to being fair.)

As Marion speaks to me, it is her utter calm that strikes me: she could not sound more relaxed, almost laconic. 'Detention was rough, of course,' she says, 'but I was fortunate that I was not physically tortured in any way, apart from the solitary confinement itself.'

After her arrest, she was kept at John Vorster Square for six months and then at Diepkloof (or 'Sun City' as it is still widely known) until her trial in November 1986. 'I was then at Pretoria Central Women's Prison, which is where all the white women political prisoners were kept,' she says.

At her trial, she found that her prosecutors could not accept that she had acted of her own volition, but were convinced that, as a woman, she must have been influenced by a man – any man. This is an echo of the Patti Hearst case in the US in 1974, in which Hearst the heiress became part of the organisation that had kidnapped her and helped them to rob a bank before being arrested. For Marion, in the end, the prosecutors fixed on her mentor, Joe Slovo.

'The trial was very brief, and I remember that one of the most traumatic things was trying to convince some of my lawyers that I was serious. People like Norman Manoim[17] and Peter Harris[18] were great, but at first some of the junior advocates seemed more concerned with whether they would have done what I did and seemed to think they had to justify themselves to me.

'They came around in the end, I think, but it was also odd, because, after my first day in the dock, it was only when Johann Kriegler, who was chairman of the Johannesburg Bar Council then and attended my trial, came up to my senior advocate and said he was impressed with my testimony that my advocate turned to me and said the same. So he needed assurance from a colleague before he took me seriously!

'In the end though, and with hindsight, I realise that my actions were a challenge to many white South Africans – and, of course, were intended to be.'

Some thirty years later, it's difficult to explain to anyone who is not South African the extraordinary impact of a white woman bombing three police stations. There was an active women's movement in South Africa during the 1970s and 1980s, but there was still a widespread expectation that white women would marry, bear children, shop, cook and look after the family as their main role over and above any career ambitions. Marion's actions shook the foundations of the white conservatives. She was one of them by virtue of her skin colour, yet she was seen by them as a *verraaier* (traitor).

When she got up in court, wearing the green, black and yellow colours of the banned ANC, and pleaded guilty, she became one of the very few white women in South Africa to be convicted of treason, and the first to be convicted of terrorist acts. She was sentenced to twenty years for the bombing of the PFP offices and five years for 'arson' – placing the three limpet mines, two of which blew the doors off the police toilets in East London and Johannesburg. She could have been hanged – the death penalty was frequently imposed in South Africa, particularly, against those who stood up against the government.

'Even some of the security police felt they somehow had to justify themselves to me,' Marion explains. 'When they were driving me to prison after the trial, one woman was trying to get under my skin and annoy me with the fact that I had a twenty-five-year sentence ahead of me.

'Her male colleague turned to her and told her to shut up and said that I would survive prison and be a lot better off than either of them. The rest of the ride to prison was silent. Strange, but silent. And then this same guy, who was driving, got lost and could not find his way there.'

Then reality hit.

'Prison after my sentence was a lot tougher than detention,' Marion says. She was kept in solitary confinement for three months for what her captors described as 'observation' – although the only thing they could 'observe', she remarks, 'was someone going crazy. I had expected to join my comrades immediately, so it was rough being on my own again.'

Once the three months were over, Marion was happy to join the other prisoners. 'The time in prison was not easy, because there was such a small group of us confined together. There were never more than five or six of us, and such a small group can really become difficult. One cannot "walk away" from issues and conflicts, and relationships become very intense at times.

'The person I became closest to in prison was Barbara [Hogan, convicted in 1982 of treason and membership of the then banned ANC], and it was a privilege to serve my time with her. She has fought so hard for many of the basic rights since her imprisonment. Barbara and I have not been able to see each other as often as we would want to since our release, but the bonds one forms in prison are unbreakable. She has a very special place in my heart and always will have. She is one of the bravest people I know and is living proof that prison cannot destroy a person's spirit and strength.'

On her release in 1991, Marion was swept off to a press conference and a series of ANC events before being reunited with her family. Then she worked for the ANC before becoming deputy executive director of the Constitutional Assembly, the body that would draft South Africa's Constitution, and later chief executive of the National Prosecuting Authority before joining the advertising agency DraftFCB, for whose social marketing division she is now strategy director.

Did you suffer post-traumatic stress?

'Yes, I was already on antidepressants when I came out of prison. There was an initial period of complete dislocation – the only word I can find to describe it.' Marion's father had died while she was in prison, and she had not seen her family for years before that, because she had been in exile.

Moreover, the South Africa she had left behind no longer existed. 'There was really no "everyday" life to return to,' she explains. 'It was a matter of forging a new life. The South Africa I left when I went into exile did not exist anymore.'

How had your parents reacted to your arrest?

'They were pretty shocked, of course. They were both arrested and treated pretty badly, so they had their own trauma to deal with. My younger sister [Debbie] was also arrested and detained. So the family had a rough time. They were magnificent, though.

'It just shows what love can achieve. They did not have the political conviction that I had to keep going. It was purely love, and a basic sense of fairness and dignity, that kept them on my side all the way through. It was rough also for them, because not all members of the bigger family responded positively to me and my actions, and they found themselves having to defend me.'

Marion's parents, Esther and Wreford, were very supportive. So much so, that when she disappeared in the aftermath of the PFP bombing (which they had no idea she was involved in), they flew to

Gaborone to try to find her. The trip was in vain; she had already left. She only found out about this trip from her mother after her release from prison.

* * *

I speak to Marion's sister Debbie, now an infrastructure project manager in Johannesburg; she had also studied at Rhodes. She says of Marion's imprisonment: 'It was quite traumatic. We didn't understand it, because she was the only one of us who was political.' Once Marion went into exile, the sisters didn't see each other for years. Later, when Debbie moved to Joburg to live and Marion was back in the country illegally, they met up. Marion had dyed her hair blonde to disguise herself. 'I knew she was involved with MK,' Debbie tells me, 'but I had no clue what she was up to. I used to meet her in Hillbrow for coffee or lunch. She told me, "The less you know, the better."'

Debbie did help Marion, renting her the car she used to transport the bombs, because the car-hire company required a credit card. She did not know Marion's plan.

After Marion's arrest, Debbie was detained too. 'I remember very clearly the day I was arrested,' she says. She was at a friend's home, watching the James Bond film *From Russia with Love*. She was taken by the police back to her own flat, where her startled flatmate arrived in the middle of the police search, and then to John Vorster Square. She was fairly well treated, she says. She was interrogated daily, but only after she had showered and had breakfast. In fact, after a few days of her arriving for interrogation with her long hair dripping wet, they gave her a hairdryer.

'There was no abuse. They played "good cop, bad cop",' she says. Oosthuizen made occasional appearances. 'He was not very pleasant. He would try to manipulate between Marion and myself, saying, "Your sister has told me everything", and insisting that I had been recruited.

'I knew I wasn't guilty of anything. My sister had been back in the country illegally; they said I should have given her up.' Debbie was far more worried about her sister, knowing she was accused of more serious offences. 'I did quite a lot of crying in my cell.'

The family found the trial very difficult, she says. 'It wasn't pleasant, and what made it harder was that Marion was hard on herself. And the judge was hard on her because she was white.'

Did you believe in what Marion did?

'Yes and no. I believed in the end goal of freedom, but I didn't agree with the means, the use of violence. I was relieved that no one was hurt. I don't know how I would have felt about it if there had been somebody killed. I was very shocked and upset about Robert McBride and the bombing of the pub Magoo's Bar[19] in Durban. Quite a few people were hurt and killed.'

Marion is very strong-willed, says Debbie. 'She stands up for what she believes in. She doesn't talk a lot about herself.' As the only close family member who was living nearby, Debbie visited Marion most often in prison.

What were her spirits like?

'Better than I expected, although she wouldn't always be happy and beaming. As time went by, she acclimatised, telling us about how they had a little garden and were growing vegetables. She made friends with one or two people, including Barbara Hogan; they kept the white political women all together.'

* * *

In Observatory, I can't resist asking Marion whether she would do it all over again. 'I can only say yes, I would,' she replies. 'Obviously there is a lot that was difficult, painful. But I am the same person and so, faced with the same challenges, I would make the same choices.'

Marion has two adopted children: Michelle and Joy. 'I always wanted a child,' she tells me.

Looking back at her time at Rhodes, she says it was Guy Berger who had the biggest influence on her: 'I aspired to be a journalist like Guy.' While at university, she had no idea that he was politically involved or she would have approached him. And the same holds for Zubeida, with whom Marion has friends in common: 'I only got to know Zubeida later, when I came out of prison. She had a really horrific time. A lot of the true horror, she hasn't been able to write about. She is a hero. A real hero.'

It's a sober moment, but as with all three activists, humour keeps resurfacing. 'One of the absurd things – this just used to crack me up every time – is that they couldn't treat me the same as a black person; it was just beyond them. Apartheid was so part of their psyche, down to the issue of food. I was in detention in John Vorster Square, arrested for all of these terrible things, and yet, I couldn't eat the same food as black detainees, because I was white. So they used to go and get the food from the police barracks for me, basically meat and three veg, because I had to eat "white food".

'One day, the poor uniformed policeman made a mistake and brought me "black food", which was basically just *pap* and a little bit of gravy and cabbage on top; it was not like the meat and vegetables that you got as a white detainee. They used to bring it to you in a polystyrene container. And I remember I opened it and thought, OK, it's not the usual kind of food they bring me, but I was about to start eating it when a policewoman rushed in and said, "No, no, we're sorry, we gave you the wrong food!"

'When you think about it, you ended up with a sentence of life imprisonment, but even if you were a terrorist, the fact is you were a white terrorist, so you had to be treated differently from a black terrorist.'

Being a white terrorist engaged in underground operations could make things somewhat easier too. With great merriment Marion tells me: 'I'd gone into John Vorster Square a couple of times before that morning [of the bombing] just to check it was going to work. But that morning when I went in with the limpets, a black policeman at the gate wanted to search me and a white policeman stopped him as I made a bit of a fuss about it, because I wasn't going to allow myself to be searched. The white policeman stopped him and said, "You can't search a white woman!"'

She warms to her theme: 'You could see the tension between the black policemen and the white policemen as well. There were a couple of times when I came back to John Vorster Square with white policemen in the vehicle, and then they were stopped at the gate by the black policemen, who obviously were just being treated as security guards. These black policemen had clearly decided it was time to make a point. They would say, "Please stop the vehicle, open the boot, I need to search it." And these white policemen would be swearing at them and saying, "It's us, it's us, you know it's us." "Please open the boot. I need to search it." "This is a dangerous terrorist." And they would say, "Please open the boot, I want to search it." It was very funny.'

Marion had found that being white was her best defence from the moment she came back into the country. 'In Lesotho, I had been put in touch with Steve Marais, who lived in the former Transkei close to the Lesotho border. He was going to help me with transport for the bombing of the Cambridge police station. He wasn't part of the bombing; in fact he knew nothing about it until afterwards. I deliberately didn't want him to know anything. I had a vehicle for East London, just for the bombing itself; when I arrived I had checked out the police station beforehand.'

She had her story planned. 'At Cambridge, I think I said I'd come to apply for a firearms licence.' Then she asked to use the toilet. 'I was very fortunate in Cambridge actually, because the toilet that the public normally would have used was apparently out of order, so they sent me into the back of the police station, all the way through the main radio control room. After arming and placing the limpet – I knew it would be about forty-five minutes before it went off – I went and picked up Steve.

'I didn't want to leave the Eastern Cape straight after the bombing, because I thought in the aftermath they'd probably put roadblocks up everywhere. So Steve and I drove down to Port Alfred.'

The two fugitives stayed at a cottage on the beach in Port Alfred, which was a popular weekend destination for Rhodes students. The little resort, called Rugged Rocks, still exists. It was February, still summer, but schools were back in session and the area was quiet.

'Then after a few days, when the coast was clear and we were sure there weren't any big roadblocks we were going to encounter, I left Steve in the Eastern Cape and drove back to Joburg.'

Her calculation was right: there were no roadblocks. The bombing had been on the news and in the newspapers, but the excitement had died down.

It must have been quite satisfying.

'Yes, it was.' She laughs. 'Because I can remember when Steve heard it on the news, he came to me and said, "Why didn't you tell me about it?" and I said, "I couldn't tell you about it; it was better that you didn't know anything about it". '

There was another reason that Marion wanted to get out of the Eastern Cape: there was a good chance that she would be recognised. Originally, she had not intended to operate there at all. And she certainly didn't want to be hitchhiking – that's why she had been given a car.

She had never planned the East London bombing; it had been a request from her commander Eddie, who had told her of the terrible treatment of some of the comrades from Lesotho at the hands of security police based in the Cambridge police station. She agreed on condition that it was the only time she operated in the Eastern Cape.

Soon Marion was in Joburg on her own, staying in Hillbrow. There were two more bombings to complete: these were the targets that she had chosen herself. The first was John Vorster Square.

'At the gate I said, "I'm coming to apply for a firearms licence." But once you were in past the gate, no one really paid any attention to where you were going or what you were doing. John Vorster Square was ten floors high. I didn't want to place the limpet on the ground floor, but I can't remember whether I made it to the first, second or third floor. I wasn't quite sure what was on all the other floors. I knew I wasn't going to be able to get all the way up to the tenth floor without people saying, "Who are you, what are you doing here?" But I think I got to the first or second floor without anyone asking me what I was doing. I didn't realise until I'd walked in that it was actually the male toilets that I was in – there was no one in there.

'And unlike Cambridge police station, the toilet was massive. It was about three times the size of this room [she gestures to the long dining room where we are sitting], and the toilets were against a whole bank of windows, so there was a window ledge that was quite high above one of the toilets. I put the limpet up there. Then I came down to Hillbrow police station and there was a ledge there too.'

So you just put the limpet up there and walked out, and you knew you had an hour. Did you walk or take a bus to Hillbrow?

'I took a bus.'

So you had the limpets in your handbag?

'Yes.'

How did that feel, going around with a limpet mine in your handbag? I suppose you knew how it worked … and that it was safe?

'Yes, and also the limpets I was using were small, like a cylinder cut in half; they almost looked like a loaf of bread. They had big ones, but the ones I was using were the small ones. They were obviously a lot easier to carry around.'

Marion is insouciant about having carried these deadly bombs from one police station to another. When she got to her next target police station, she didn't even bother with the firearms licence excuse.

'Because Hillbrow was such a small place, I simply walked in and asked where the Ladies was.

'But the Hillbrow one didn't go off. I didn't realise that, because when they arrested me it was only when *I* mentioned it that someone said, "Oh *and* Hillbrow!"'

Marion laughs. 'And my flat was only two blocks away from the Hillbrow police station, so half of them suddenly rushed off out of my place and found the unexploded limpet still there. I suppose something had gone wrong with the detonator.'

So if you hadn't told them?

'Probably they would never have found it.'

So thanks to her, the police knew about the second Johannesburg bomb, but only much later did they find out that she had bombed the East London police station too.

'They didn't link me to East London for a while,' Marion says. 'But I had already decided how I was going to handle my case: that I was going to plead guilty.'

Today, Marion would have been captured on CCTV after the first bomb, and her image would immediately have been flashed up on TV screens and online all around the country. In all likelihood, she would have been caught before she'd had the chance to place the other two limpets.

The trial took place in November 1986. It was almost exactly six months after her arrest, Marion explains, because there was a legal requirement to bring prisoners to trial within six months, unless an extension was granted. As she pleaded guilty, her trial only took two days.

Although Marion has nothing but praise for her trial lawyers, her decision to plead guilty did puzzle her advocate Jules Browde. 'He thought I was being reckless. He said it was OK for me to plead guilty, but basically I must say I'm sorry. I said to him, "No, I'm not going to say I'm sorry just to get a lesser sentence. It's not my objective to get a lesser sentence." So *ja*, it was a bit difficult arguing with him for a while.

'But in the end he understood. He battled with the issue of violence, and at one stage told me that Oliver Tambo did not agree with the use of violence. I could have got really angry but I just smiled at him and said, "Jules, I am not saying sorry for what I did, because I am not".'

Eric Pelser, a young man whose trial was held just before Marion's, had pleaded guilty and apologised, saying he had been misled. Jules had defended him too. 'And the security police – apparently when they found out I was pleading guilty, they also assumed I was going to say, "I'm sorry, I was misled" and try to avoid a lengthy sentence.'

Marion's lifelong friend Alison Gillwald, a fellow Rhodes journalism graduate, gave evidence on her behalf. Her own family, however, was subpoenaed to appear for the prosecution.

'They wanted to refuse. But I told them to accept the flights from the prosecution and come up, and then they could be there for the trial. I knew they wouldn't have to appear as I planned to plead guilty. I also knew that if they refused to appear for the prosecution, they would be arrested.'

On her day in court, there was no pretence that there was an 'independent' prosecutor. 'The security policeman Oosthuizen was sitting next to the prosecutor, on the same bench during my trial, and when the prosecutor realised I wasn't saying sorry, he turned and looked at Oosthuizen with complete exasperation, like, "What the hell do I do now? This person's not saying sorry! Now I'm going to have to rethink my whole strategy".'

There was a paucity of witnesses, says Marion. Nobody had been injured in any of the bombings, and all the prosecution could muster were several policemen and a civilian, 'who was required to say that he had been scared'.

A letter to her mother found on her when she was arrested was quite strangely presented as evidence against her. This technique boomeranged and ended up supporting Marion's strategy at trial. The prosecution had been briefed by Oosthuizen to expect an apology from Marion and planned to use it as proof of just how committed a terrorist she was. The letter read:

Dear Mom,

It is not an easy task for me to explain myself in a letter like this, but I am going to try; so just bear with me as I stumble along ... I can understand that in a way you have cause to resent me, for bringing more pain and problems to a family that has already had more than its fair share of trouble. I know also that I have to work out how to survive on my own without depending on anyone. And I believe I am doing all I can at the moment ...

Yes, I do feel sad at not being able to be with you and the family. But I do not regret giving up my previous life. I do not regret the commitment I have made. The struggle to get this country free now is my life. If I did not truly believe in what I am doing I would have succumbed to a nervous breakdown or some form of insanity a long time ago. I don't really expect you or Dad to agree fully with my actions. But I did have an idea that you understood a little. I value the past four or five years more than you could know. The people I have met, the experiences I have gone through, I believe have made me a more complete person. My life has meaning now. I know where I am going and I know we will reach there – even if I don't personally make it. I have never been more fulfilled. This is probably sounding very trite, but I hope it conveys something of the depth and understanding I've gained over the past few years.

Daily happenings only serve to increase my determination and, I am afraid, harden me a little each day. In Alexandra last week, more than 80 people were shot dead. Most were simply teenagers with nothing more than stones in their hands. But I can understand the fear of the white policemen and soldiers as they faced those children. I can understand their fear as they failed to understand how children with stones were prepared to take on armoured cars and submachine guns. But anyway, I'm not going to give you a lecture on that. I do get very bitter and angry still, but what these past years have given me is confidence and hope – the knowledge that we will win. The government knows it too. They are only prolonging the agony for all – black and white. It is the people who give me hope – not only those kids in Alexandra and elsewhere. But especially the individuals I've met – black and white. I've been able to discover what real friendship, love and trust are all about. I know our future is safe in their hands.

I think it is natural for a child to want to make its parents proud. And although it is hard for you to understand, let alone feel proud, I hope one day, if time is kind, you will be able to understand and feel proud. I know it.

If you could meet the people and know the people I am close to, you would understand. Do you remember the young white guy who was killed in the SADF [South African Defence Force] raid on Gaborone? Well, his parents said afterwards they never understood until they went to his funeral and met all his friends and those who worked with him.

They said only then they realised how much he meant to others, and that his life was good and worthwhile, even if they still couldn't accept all his actions completely. I only hope it doesn't have to take death to bring you to that understanding. And in any case I have made enemies of my family and some previous friends. For if they are to defend apartheid then I am their enemy for life. It is painful but true. But it is not all that surprising, for South Africa is in a state of war. And war turns brother against brother, and father against son. You see, there is really no going back for me. Neither can I stand still. We can only move forward now.

If it means my life I am quite prepared. In fact, I'd be proud to be counted among those who fought and died for this country and people.

This is probably sounding very romantic and reckless, but then it is very difficult to put down in words the simple yet profound principles of one's life. If I were to live like a 'mole', that is part of the price that must be paid. And it is a very small price compared to what others have gone through, and are still going through.

I suppose the one thing I really need to talk to you about is wanting to have a child. I've met and loved other men – and especially one now whose child I would be proud to have. But I know there is no time. I want to be able to be with my child all the time. And now there is so much else to do. I had virtually made up my mind that I was going to have a child no matter what. And then there was the SADF raid on Lesotho in December last year, where, among others, a young white woman and her coloured husband were killed. They were shot dead in bed.

Their one-year-old daughter lay screaming next to their bodies until neighbours came to fetch her. Then I thought, God!

I don't want my baby to have to go through that. And yet, the baby will have cause to be proud one day. So who knows, maybe I will be lucky enough to have a child.

I don't know if I have gone any way towards trying to explain myself. I hope some makes sense to you. In the end you'll see, it will be for the good of all. This war has to be fought to the bitter end. And it is going to be bitter. I have no illusions about that. But in the end, there will be a happier life for all of us – black and white. And I quite honestly believe that this is going to happen in our lifetime, not that of our children or grandchildren.

Just know that I do love you even if you feel exasperated, betrayed or hurt.

Yours,

Marion

There are many accounts of Marion's trial. But one in the *Philadelphia Inquirer*, by the journalist David Zucchino (now in Afghanistan for the *Los Angeles Times*) struck me as touching in its attention to the detail of that day:

Yesterday morning, Sparg stood silently before Justice P.J. van der Walt, her blond hair tumbling over her shoulders. She wore a green blouse, black suit and yellow scarf – the colors of the outlawed African National Congress.

The judge stared down over his spectacles at her as he laid out the life history of the only white South African woman ever trained as a guerrilla by the military wing of the ANC. Sparg had become only the third white South African woman ever convicted of treason, and the very first convicted of terrorist acts.

31

After 18 minutes of somber detail, the judge pronounced the sentence: 20 years for treason and five years for arson, for a total of 25 years in prison.

Sparg looked up at Van der Walt, but said nothing. After a moment, she peered back over her shoulder at her supporters, both black and white, in the packed gallery of the Rand Supreme Court. They waved yellow chrysanthemums at her, and she waved and smiled back at them.

Her mother and father smiled weakly at her. It could have been worse. Treason is punishable by death in South Africa, although the prosecution had asked only for life imprisonment.

Just two months ago, three young black men of the ANC were hanged in Pretoria after being convicted of terrorism and murder. Van der Walt mentioned that the two white women convicted of treason before Sparg got 10 years in prison each.

The judge also pointed out that, 'providentially,' no one had been injured by Sparg's firebombs and limpet mines.

'Had lives been lost, you would have almost certainly received a death sentence,' he told her.

And, though the judge said he considered her motives 'misguided,' he added: 'The court accepts that you are sincere in your beliefs. I respect your frankness.'

Sparg nodded stiffly. She seemed resigned, but also defiant. She said she long ago had proffered herself as a willing martyr for the anti-apartheid cause.

'I believe that even as a white South African, I do not owe any loyalty to a government that is clearly not based on the will of its people,' Sparg testified Monday.

Because she pleaded guilty, her trial lasted only two days. In that time, she was able to lay out in a bold and articulate manner the reasons for her actions.

She was trained as a journalist at Rhodes University, but lasted less than a year at the *Sunday Times* of Johannesburg. She did not consider journalists neutral observers of volatile events in South Africa; her editors did.

'I had had enough of the so-called liberal white press in this country,' Sparg testified.

She rejected her family and the rest of white South Africa and struck out against apartheid on her own. 'I felt disillusioned by the lack of commitment in white politics,' she told the court.

Her first act of violence was aimed at a peculiar target: the Johannesburg offices of the Progressive Federal Party (PFP), the anti-apartheid political opposition of the government. In all, she firebombed three PFP offices in 1981.

In court, Sparg said she now regretted attacking the PFP. She said her political attitudes at the time were 'immature.' They soon would harden, she testified.

In court, Sparg said she set the bombs to explode at noon on busy weekdays. She intended to injure police officers because they were agents of apartheid, she said.

'I am a soldier. I follow orders like any other soldier,' she testified Monday.

'So the police are combatants, too, and must look after themselves?' the judge asked her.

'... You are a mature and intelligent young woman,' he told her. 'You have suffered no particular hardships in your life. Yet you have chosen to align yourself against law and order in your own country.'

Had she been black, the judge said, he could have comprehended, though not condoned, her actions. 'The fact that as a white South African you chose to espouse the cause of revolution I regard as an aggravating feature of this case,' he said.

Sparg was no ordinary criminal who could be rehabilitated, the judge went on. 'Your acts deserve severe punishment,' he told her.

... [Sparg] accepted her sentence mutely and turned to hug and kiss her family and supporters.

She gave a black power handshake to one of her attorneys, a bespectacled white man dressed in long black barrister's robes. Someone handed her a bouquet of yellow chrysanthemums.

White police officers armed with pistols and the leather truncheons called sjamboks rose to escort her from the courtroom. Sparg took no notice of them.

A black woman in the gallery shouted 'Amandla!' three times – Power! Power! Power! The police stared hard at her, but did nothing. One of them snorted in contempt.

Mr. and Mrs. E.A. Sparg and their daughters Judy and Debbie said goodbye to Marion. Mrs. Sparg, a white-haired woman in a tan suit, was weeping. Her husband, a tall man who walked with a limp, was not.

Marion Sparg, her face flushed, waved once more to the gallery, and then she was gone. A police officer escorted her gingerly down a side corridor to her jail cell, careful not to muss her flowers.

Her parents watched their daughter leave the court as she had once left them, an outcast and revolutionary. Silently, they linked arms with their remaining daughters, heads raised and speaking to no one, and walked outside into a cold morning rain.

And so Marion began a twenty-five-year sentence. If she hadn't been white (and a woman), she may well have been hanged, like some of her compatriots.

That year, on a visit to Cape Town, I stood staring at a three-feet-high graffito on a wall around the corner from my old house in Rondebosch: VIVA SPARG.

* * *

Just before my meeting in Johannesburg with Marion, I had read Peter Harris's *In a Different Time,* about the four ANC cadres who were prepared to pay the ultimate price for fighting the system, written by their lawyer.

My publisher, Maggie Davey, used to go and visit them years ago on

34

death row, I tell Marion. Maggie had told me that Ting Ting [Masango] always used to ask whether Marion was bearing up, because at that time she was in prison facing a life sentence, and he couldn't get any information.

The links between the Delmas Four and Marion were strong. After her release in 1991, Marion was asked within days by Peter Harris to go visit them. 'I was quite horrified,' she admits. 'I mean, the last thing I wanted to do was to go back into prison, particularly as they were on death row at the time. It was pretty harrowing, but at the same time I realised it was important for them that I did go to see them.'

Sadly, Ting Ting Masango, the biggest personality of all, died of complications from diabetes in 2009. 'Ting Ting was the one who always managed to remain the most cheerful, no matter what situation he found himself in. He was on death row, and yet, when I walked in to meet him, he had the biggest smile on his face and he didn't stop smiling, not once during the visit,' says Marion.

The Delmas Four had left South Africa after the 1976 riots; Marion had met Ting Ting in Caxito. After training with the MK, Ting Ting returned with Jabu Masina, Neo Potsane and Joseph Makhura in 1985 to carry out the bombings.

They were arrested ten months later, but elected to remain silent during their trial, refusing to participate in the process as they wanted to be tried as prisoners of war and MK soldiers. They were found guilty and sentenced to death. At first, they refused to appeal against their sentences, but were persuaded by the ANC to do so at the eleventh hour, and they were released after eighteen months when they staged a hunger strike. After a stint in broadcasting, Ting Ting became an ANC member of Parliament.

These are only four of the fighters that Marion met while training in Angola. However, in their courage and their convictions, they are representative of the vast number of idealists who fled the country.

Marion continues her story: 'The impression I got after I'd been through the whole arrest and interrogation and everything was that –

and I mean, you can only say this with hindsight – the security police didn't know a quarter of what I thought they had known, so they were not so well informed. They had lots of information, but they didn't have lots of accurate information, and they didn't know how to put it together to make sense of it.'

In any case, there was not a huge amount of information that she could give away. 'It sounds so horribly matter-of-fact the way I say it now, but there'd been the second Maseru killings,[20] which had happened months before I was arrested, and quite literally everyone – with the exception of two people – everyone I was in contact with in Maseru had been killed. There wasn't anyone I could expose in Lesotho – because they were all dead.'

This is said in such a flat tone, yet with such feeling.

Today Marion is strategy director at the social marketing division of DraftFCB, which runs campaigns to drive behaviour change in areas such as electricity theft, job creation, prevention of HIV infection, and violence against women and children in South Africa. It's part of a global entity and the oldest advertising agency in South Africa, but the division itself is barely five years old, pioneering a new approach in the country. The work has, in its aims, a close fit with Marion's early life and convictions.[21]

We have reached the end of our time together. I had promised to take Marion and the girls out for a meal. First I photograph them with their Alsatian in the garden, on the carpet of fallen jacaranda blossoms. Then we drive to the restaurant in her big BMW four-by-four.

The girls are excited and giggly. We sit outside; we talk; they try on my sunglasses and take photographs with my iPhone; we eat. Marion and I talk about Zuma, whom she has seen recently.

Then it is over. Marion and the girls leave, I call the taxi-driver who dropped me at her house, and I am back at my B&B.

That night I go out with my friend Rob to a vegetarian restaurant – which, had the doors not been wide open to the hot night air of the street, might well have been in Camden. 'You must realise,' he says before we fall hungrily upon the polenta, the stuffed mushrooms and the vegan smoothies, 'that at any point tonight a car could squeal to a halt outside, and six men with machine guns could run in and rob us all.' He grins. 'I love it here.'

That afternoon we had made a tour of his old haunts – the mansion he grew up in Parkhurst; his old school, a massive, moneyed sprawl of land and buildings; and neighbourhoods that had been open land, where he roamed with his friends. After twenty years in Britain and Belgium, he returned in 2006 with the Homecoming Revolution.[22] He lived first in Cape Town, where he ran an organic food business, and then, missing the buzz of his birthplace, moved back to Joburg. He's just had his car stolen. But he doesn't seem to mind, not in the least.

Johnny Clegg is singing in Joburg that night – it's a big outdoor gig. I am keen to go; Rob isn't. 'I don't like Johnny Clegg,' he says. 'I'll drop you there if you like.' I pass. A big outdoor event, at night and on my own, having already been robbed in broad daylight? No thanks. I've already failed the tourist test.

PART TWO

Guy Berger

THE NEXT DAY I FLY TO PORT ELIZABETH.

On the plane I am deep in thought about the 1980s. For those who were born in a free South Africa, and for those who are accustomed to a First World democracy, it is difficult to comprehend what the political situation in South Africa was like at that time.

It was 1981, five years after the 1976 Soweto uprising. The white population had sunk back into its happy stupor. The combination of strict censorship, geographic separation and pass laws meant that, in general, the only black people that white people met were their servants.

The Brixton riots[23] in the UK in 1981 drew comment from the comfortable homes of well-off white South Africans. That year I made a trip from the UK to Cape Town for a wedding, and more than once I found myself under verbal attack for having left South Africa for a country that had its own race riots. Tasteless jokes would fly around the lunch table as the servants silently cleared plates, summoned by the imperative tinkle of the brass bell that stood by my mother-in-law's place at the head of the table.

I'm ashamed to say I was largely quiet on these occasions. Not because I didn't have strong opinions – I did, and occasionally I expressed them in print – but because the views of my parents-in-law were so very far from my own. In a nearby restaurant, our waitress apologised profusely for the fact that they hadn't been able to have the *magrets de canard* flown in from France that week. There was some problem with the supplier, she said. I was appalled. The previous week, there had been a protest shooting in a church just up the road; nearby there were thousands of people starving. Meanwhile, we sat choosing from a menu of imported luxury items.

I recall ringing my mother-in-law some years later. I had just seen tanks rolling into the townships on the BBC's *Nine O'Clock News*.

'Are you OK, Mom?'

'No, the place is in an uproar!'

'Yes, we know – we were worried.'

'Yes. It's the All Blacks – they're not coming!'[24]

In a sense, she was hardly to be blamed. Like many, she lived in a white bubble made impervious by her wealth. She had grown up in Paarl, a rural town where apartheid attitudes were so entrenched that black men and women had to get off the pavement and walk on the road if a white person was approaching.

However, like many Afrikaners, she was kind to her servants, although she was a deeply religious Dutch Reformed worshipper and believed in the apartheid credo taken from the Bible that the sons of Ham 'were drawers of water and hewers of wood'. (For 'sons of Ham', read 'the black population'.)

The world I had grown up in was subtly different. My parents voted for the United Party,[25] although my publisher father explained that because the voting districts were rigged by the Nationalists, their local candidate was unlikely to get into Parliament; our vote in Rondebosch was counted in a district miles away. Nevertheless, at age ten, I questioned him crossly: 'Why aren't we in charge? Because then we would do away with apartheid?' And: 'There are more of us – aren't there?' By 'us', I meant 'English-speaking liberals'. To my small, angry self, it seemed there *were* more of us. That's because I lived in a comfortable little white, English-speaking enclave.

My father laughed out loud. 'Two-thirds of the white population are Afrikaans – only one-third is English.' It was one of the biggest shocks of my childhood. We were outnumbered!

To my child's brain, unaware of the freedom struggle that was in full swing in the 1970s, the other possibility for change lay outside South Africa – the actions of other countries. And particularly the UK, where a Labour government put pressure on the apartheid government, while a Conservative government did not. I listened anxiously to the election results on our transistor radio every four years. I scanned the newspapers, the *Cape Times* and the *Cape Argus*, and, when it came, *Time* magazine, our only real window on the outside world, a world outside a country that was subject not so much to censorship as to complete information lockdown.

And, of course, unwittingly, I was part of the history of this time myself. As a child aged six, I took part with my classmates in a Nazi-style parade at the Goodwood Showgrounds to celebrate the fifth anniversary of South Africa's leaving the British Commonwealth.

My education, at a rather academic, serious girls' school that was the oldest in the Cape, was affected too. Forced to take history in high school (art was not, apparently, academic enough), I imbibed, unwillingly, the lies and propaganda that made up the syllabus. It was illegal to talk about the truth or otherwise of these events, so our history teacher, Miss Simpson, told us that she would simply write them out on the blackboard and proceeded to do so. We girls rolled our eyes and got our pens out. It was also decided that we did not receive enough religious instruction, so another RI lesson was introduced every morning between assembly and classes. Our class teacher was as furious as we were and announced that she would read us Bunyan's *Pilgrim's Progress* every morning. We were free to listen, put our heads on our arms and sleep, or read something else entirely – it was our choice.

We lived a privileged life, quietly serviced by servants. I remember being shocked to find out that while our schoolbooks were free, black people had to pay for their children's books. How did that make sense? And, of course, we weren't unaware that the women who made our beds and did our cooking were separated from their own children,

40

who were not allowed to live with them in the backyards of our family homes in the 'maid's room' and were often looked after hundreds of miles away by their grandparents. Our own domestic worker, Beauty (the english version of her name) once brought her small daughter to stay for a few days. She was lively, voluble and engaging. A teenager by then, I was utterly charmed by her and spent some time trying to teach her to read. Then she disappeared back to the Ciskei. I wondered how her mother must have felt.

In 1976, I was in my matric year when the Soweto uprising began. There were, of course, protests in Cape Town too – and at my school, not a little unease. The Sharpeville massacre[26] in 1966 had prompted a flood of whites to leave the country, something our parents remembered. We were distressed at the stories filtering through to us of police shootings of children. Some of us had been through the edges of those crowds on our way to or from school and had glimpsed some of the consequent anger. We had small tales of fright to tell, most of which came to nothing. One of my friends and her mother were caught up in a line of cars as young people streamed by. As they sat there, my friend said, a boy lifted a rock over his head in both hands, ready to bring it down on their windscreen. Then he caught her eye, lowered the rock, smiled at her and ran off. My mother and I, taking our domestic worker home to Gugulethu one afternoon, caught a small rock on the wing mirror of the car on our way home. It made a neat, round, deep hole, a tiny reminder of what was happening outside our cosy enclave.

My route when horse-riding after school took me past the edges of a few settlements. Now and then, out in the bush, a shower of pebbles would land on the horse's rump from an unseen source, making him skitter sideways. Fair enough, I thought; I would do the same. Once I took a short cut down a dirt road to get home. I was feeling self-conscious: the horse, although he wasn't mine, was a clear symbol of white wealth. There were stares; a woman bent down and picked up a rock. She threw it with force. I flinched instinctively, but there was a yelp from the dog she had aimed at – a dog that was coming up behind us, teeth bared. There were plenty of dogs along those trails, and I soon learned to turn the horse and gallop straight at them to make them turn tail. My mother began to insist that, although I much preferred riding alone, I was to go out in company.

The previous December, my sister had got married. When I look at the wedding photographs now, I see a microcosm of the white middle-class reaction to apartheid. There I am in my sprigged Laura Ashley bridesmaid's dress, standing next to my brother-in-law's two best friends: the best man, Anton Eberhard, was to be imprisoned for refusing to be called up, the first to refuse the draft on political grounds; and the groomsman, Dr Ivan Toms, whose defiance of the SADF and the apartheid system, his creation of a medical clinic in Crossroads, his hunger strike, and his imprisonment for refusing further army service would cause Archbishop Tutu to say at his funeral service in St George's Cathedral in 2008: 'I thank God that I knew him. Knowing him makes [one] feel proud. This is a prime example of someone who had *ubuntu*.[27] He was utterly selfless.' Ivan had died unexpectedly of meningitis; he was just fifty-four years old. But in his lifetime, he had done more than most: he had engaged wholeheartedly with the struggle.[28]

Anton, now a professor at the University of Cape Town working in energy research, tells me: 'I received a call-up for a military training camp in 1977. I wrote to my commanding officer and the minister of defence, Magnus Malan, informing them that I was refusing my call-up as I considered the South African Army's role to be illegitimate. Only whites were conscripted, and the army's role was to defend the apartheid state.

'Troops were being deployed in black townships and also across our borders in Namibia and Angola. I was arrested later that year and sentenced to twelve months in military detention barracks, ten months of which were suspended.

'I spent December 1977 and January 1978 in the Voortrekkerhoogte detention barracks in Pretoria, part of it in solitary confinement.

42

Ironically, among my fellow inmates were Cuban prisoners of war captured by the South Africans in Angola.

'I got off relatively lightly, as I was the first political conscientious objector and they didn't really know what to do with me. Later, the Conscientious Objector Support Group and the End Conscription Campaign [ECC] were established as the number of conscientious objectors grew.' By 1983, the mandatory sentence for refusing call-up was increased from two to six years. The movement gathered momentum until, in 1988, just before the ECC was banned by the government, 143 men refused to serve, followed by 771 men the following year – a public relations disaster for the government. In 1990, after Mandela's release, conscription ended.[29]

In the late eighties, I had begun writing about South Africa when I could, for one or other national paper, notably *The Guardian*. And back in South Africa after Mandela's release, it was for *The Guardian* that I wrote a piece commissioned by my former boss, city editor Alex Brummer.

He asked me to write about the economic policy of the African National Congress, newly installed as the Government of National Unity after years in the wilderness. '*What* economic policy?' I enquired. 'Precisely!' he answered.

It turned into a nightmare quest: no one from the ANC would talk to me, and I certainly could not locate an ANC economist. I was required to write out my questions and fax them to headquarters – somewhat like the old regime, I thought.

I struggled on. No answers came. David Beresford, the South African correspondent, explained that the ANC saw *The Guardian* as on its side and, therefore, felt no particular need to woo it.

Eventually, I rang Alex, and we agreed to run the story as it was, explaining that there had been no replies. The article began: 'Looking for an ANC economist is rather like hunting the snark. After a while, you begin to doubt it exists.'

Not surprisingly, this went down like a lead balloon with the ANC

– but was hugely popular with the National Party, whose newspapers picked up the story from *The Guardian* and splashed it over their front pages. Even the opposition English press picked it up and did likewise.

The day it was published, my fax machine chattered into life and spat out 20 pages of carefully typed replies to my questions – from the London office of the ANC. Then I had a call and was ordered to come to the ANC Conference at Stellenbosch, an hour from Cape Town, for an interview with that elusive creature, an ANC economist.

I manoeuvred my pregnant bump behind the wheel of a borrowed car and set off, not without a hint of nervousness. As I entered the pool house of the hotel for our meeting, he threw down a copy of *Die Burger* on the table between us and said, 'I've got a bone to pick with you!'

It was a good interview. I told him I felt passionately that economic policy was where the new South Africa would succeed or fail, that I meant everything I had said, that I had left the country twenty years before because I didn't want to live under a white Afrikaner government. I published a follow-up piece. And, of course, this was only the beginning of the process for the ANC. Trevor Manuel and Tito Mboweni worked with Thabo Mbeki to create a liberal (some have said too liberal) open market policy that reassured international markets and delivered strong economic growth to the new democracy.

The next day, Julian, our son Dominic and I were invited out to the farm of old neighbours of his from Blouberg. I sat in the cabin of a giant combine harvester and talked politics with Kosie – or was it Eduard? – as it cut swathes through their hectares of corn.

Later, a relative of theirs dropped by as we had tea. He and I stood talking by the pool. I was barefoot, holding my toddler on my hip. He mentioned the article he had seen in *Die Burger* – about how some English journalist had said the ANC's economic policy stank: 'I'd like to meet the man what wrote that article,' he said in his fractured English. I couldn't resist. 'You're looking at her,' I said gleefully, shifted Dom to the other hip, and began to explain.

It was worth it for the look on his face.

Now, twenty years on, I feel I am travelling back to that time. I am on my way to Grahamstown to see Guy Berger, now head of the journalism department where he once studied, before he was arrested and detained as a postgraduate student. I share a cab from the airport to Grahamstown with a young black boy who was returning after a family funeral to St Andrew's, one of Grahamstown's elite schools. Our driver is a former sheep farmer, once the owner of several hundred beautiful hectares, which he points out wistfully to us as we drive by. You could find no sharper delineation of how South Africa has changed politically and economically: a black pupil at an exclusive, formerly whites-only school; and a white man, once a landowner, driving a taxi.

The wide tree-lined streets of Grahamstown welcome me like an old friend. The taxi driver and I identify Guy and Jeanne Berger's house by the life-sized zebra painted on the garage door. In the early evening, Guy suggests a sunset walk. So we climb over the stile across the road from his house and wander across fields and a stream into the leafy university campus. Originally designed by Sir Herbert Baker, it has trebled in size since 1980. My old residence – John Kotze House – is still there; many new houses bear the names of heroes of the resistance.

After Joburg, Grahamstown is a little piece of heaven. While relaxing by the Bergers' pool, I photograph Guy's letters from jail. I bomb around town in Guy's old Toyota. After the theft at the Joburg airport, I am now several hundred rands poorer. Characteristically kind, Guy says: 'Don't hire a car. I'll use my bike to get in to work – it will do me good.'

Some evenings, I cook for Guy and Jeanne on their return from work. We switch on the tape recorder after supper, their brindle cat purring on the sofa as we talk of past terrors. I take them to supper at a restaurant in town, and the university's vice chancellor, Dr Saleem Badat, comes by to say hello. When he leaves, Guy leans over and tells me: 'He was badly tortured by the old regime.'

Saleem also knows Zubeida; he shared a house with her in the eighties. And that was how I came up with my maxim of the trip:

'The six degrees of Zubeida'. Never mind Kevin Bacon, somehow there was always a connection to Zubeida. In Grahamstown, I meet the woman whose house Zubeida had lived in when Rhodes University cravenly gave in to the apartheid regime that told them to create separate residences for their black students. The woman runs a café on High Street and her serious face breaks into a huge smile when I mention Zubeida. We sit at a table and she tells me what she remembers about the courageous girl who would not let the university authorities tell her what to do – who, when the university asked her to run a new black residence, simply went off campus and found a place of her own instead.

I drive down to a friend's house in Kenton-on-Sea, glimpsing the giraffes of the Kariega game reserve appearing from the mist and wildebeest gathering around a waterhole like a mirage. It underlines the privilege that still exists, and that is still largely white-owned: Kenton and neighbouring Bushman's River and Port Alfred are a bit of paradise, where English-speaking whites have built big, comfortable houses to spend the Christmas holidays with their extended families, riding on the beach, watching the sunset, braaiing, eating at the fish restaurants on the river.

The Eastern Cape is home to some of South Africa's best game parks, where you can see the 'Big Five' – lion, elephant, buffalo, rhino, and leopard – in luxury surroundings: Pumba, with its white lions; Shamwari; and Kariega on the Bushman's River. Along the coast you may, if you are lucky, add another two giants that will make it the 'Big Seven': great white sharks and whales. A short drive away is the picturesque mountain village of Hogsback. Add to that fly-fishing, hunting, hang-gliding, mountaineering, river-rafting, abseiling and skydiving, and it's a tourist's paradise, yet it is still home to desperate poverty.

I eat a late, solitary lunch, watching the sun glittering on the estuary, and remember a trip I made long ago with a fellow journalism student who was in the Rhodes rowing team. We went down to the Bushman's River for a race. I had accepted the lift only to get out of the heat of

Grahamstown on the weekend. But the Rhodes team lost in the first heat, and as a result the two of us sat talking all day. By the end of the day, I had stood up the boy I had a date with that night and had gone out with this student instead. (The boy started dating the girl who was to become my best friend; I eventually married the rower who had lost his race. But that's another story.)

At Rhodes I take off on foot, walking around the campus, through the white arch that leads to High Street, around the green gardens, down to the disused chapel where, in the unearthly quiet and the rainbow sunlight that filters through the stained-glass windows, I first encountered yoga, thanks to another journalism student, Jenny Still.

I sit in the library, going through old copies of *Grocott's Mail*, the town newspaper, the *Rhodian*, the student newspaper, and *Oppidan*, the independent student paper, looking for reports of Guy, Zubeida and Marion.

Grahamstown has changed. You would no longer amble through the town with your friends late at night, as I did years ago. I am told to keep the wrought-iron gates to the house locked and to put on the burglar alarm. Jeanne tells me that she came into the kitchen late one night when Guy was away and found a would-be intruder kneeling outside the full-length window, digging away at the putty with a knife. 'I don't know who was more startled – him or me,' she says. There's high unemployment and as sharp a divide as ever between privileged students and their lecturers, and the poorer townspeople. There have also been some brutal murders of farmers in the region.

But people are living there and many are living well. At the airport a week later, bound for Cape Town, I fall into conversation with a young woman while waiting for my flight. She is English, an Oxford graduate who fell in love with a South African farmer. Now she lives in the Eastern Cape and runs a tour company. 'I've been mugged twice,' she tells me. 'Both times in London.'

47

* * *

Guy Berger, who became head of the journalism department where he was studying in 1979, was the link between Marion and Zubeida; both admired him. I remember him as an honours student, slightly older than me, rather handsome, well liked. I knew him slightly – in our last year he shared a house with my best friend, Barbara McCrea (who went out with the boy I stood up).

Guy grew up on a smallholding just outside Johannesburg. 'My parents were fairly conservative and fairly racist,' he says, 'but because they were a bit different – my mother was Australian and my father was Lithuanian – I grew up slightly differently to other white South Africans. I didn't have roots in England or in Afrikanerdom; that meant that although my parents were happy with South Africa, they weren't the same as everyone else. I think it predisposed me to being open to different ideas and going against the grain.'

Guy owes the start of his political education to two girls at his school. He tells me that when he was fourteen, 'I asked my father who he was planning to vote for and he said the Nationalists.[30] So I graffitied "Vote Nat" on a chalkboard at school – then two liberal girls told me what it stood for.' Another clue to the reality of life under apartheid came unashamedly from his mother, who employed domestic workers from the Transkei because, she explained to him, they didn't have passes[31] and were, therefore, more docile as servants. 'One woman who worked for us had a child with the gardener who hailed from Malawi, and she also had other children, forced by the pass laws to remain in the Transkei, but who came to stay with her from time to time.' The difference between the children was marked, he says. 'The children who grew up [in the Transkei] in conditions of rural poverty were older, but were very stunted, malnourished – and not nearly as bright and alert as the Johannesburg-born child. There I was seeing this and realising that my mother was taking advantage of the pass-law system: have a quiescent worker and you can pay them less.'

48

If Guy had, as a teenager, begun to question the world he was growing up in, the next stage of his life was a real eye-opener. He became one of the thousands of conscripts who did national service each year, and in 1975 he was sent to help map southern Angola – a year before the 'official' and secret invasion by the South African army. 'We had to find paths through the swamps. They sent us out to inspect the whole terrain, with strict instructions to kill anybody we saw – woman, child or man.'

Guy was shocked by the instruction. 'I was a bit of a pacifist then, not political, but not sure why I was supposed to be killing innocent people two countries away from my own country.' He was also astonished by 'how useless the whole system was. They told us we had to put crescent-shaped claymore mines around these camps. Nobody knew which way they should point, so we put some facing in and some facing out.' He laughs. 'And the very people who did this would often, in their sense of superiority, object to doing jobs that they called "kaffir's work" in the army.'

It was the John Vorster[32] era. 'There was huge paranoia about Communists. The army told us conscripts that butterfly emblems sewn on jeans were part of the Communist onslaught – they would go from flower to flower, regardless of colour. People wearing this fashion were in line to be beaten up. These kinds of experiences made me realise that narrow-minded white people running the show was not the way it should be. The whole culture was one of a siege mentality, combining paranoia, racial arrogance and brutality.'

He arrived at Rhodes University in 1977. 'It was a mind-opening experience. You had grown up with black people as servants, and now you would meet them as equals. This was not so much on campus, which was still largely racially exclusive, but there were township activists prepared to work with left-wing white students. I met young people who were militant and proud of themselves; they educated me. It was the Black Consciousness era. They were being brave and standing up for their rights; they were out of the ghetto. At the same time, one could learn about Marxism, which was banned because its methodology was used for analysing the fusion of apartheid and capitalism, and advocating a socialist alternative.'

The Black Consciousness Movement had been formed in the wake of the banning of the ANC and the Pan Africanist Congress (PAC),[33] and echoed the rise of Black Power in the US. Despite its leader Steve Biko's own support for non-violent action, influenced by Mahatma Gandhi, it leaned towards more militant and radical solutions. Most of its key leaders were banned by 1976, the year before Biko's death.

After Biko's death, five Rhodes students, who were friends of Guy's, were involved in a big township stayaway.[34] Two white students were banned,[35] and two others gave state evidence and got off without punishment. In contrast, a black lecturer was imprisoned for his involvement and – incredibly, from today's perspective – one black scholar was caned as punishment. These events were deeply radicalising for the second-year journalism and politics student.

'For me at the time,' says Guy, 'it seemed that there wasn't an easy middle way. The Progressive Federal Party was so marginal to change, whereas so many immediate battles were going on right on the doorstep. I had to get involved directly. The only way the apartheid nut could be cracked was through direct challenge, rather than through the all-white Parliament.

'One of the things that made me more militant was when the banned crusading editor Donald Woods had to flee the country in 1977, and three newspapers were banned: the *Voice*, the *World* and the *Weekend World*.[36] To me, they had been an educational resource, enabling me to better understand what was going on in the country. Broadcasting [which was state controlled] was all sewn up by the government; other newspapers weren't as independent as Woods's *Daily Dispatch*.

'Besides making me angry about the suppression of the press, it also confirmed a hunch. This was that when you have credible information resources closed, you couldn't believe anything that was allowed to continue to be published. Your rule of thumb was to assume that whatever was reported, the opposite must then be true.'

Guy also contextualises his politicisation in terms of exposure to an anti-establishment ethos in the white student movement at the time, which in turn had been inspired in part by student protests in France and the US in the 1960s, and by the legacy of South African white student resistance to the racial segregation of universities. 'The whole atmosphere gave you an alternative way of seeing and a chance to liberate yourself from the narrow identity prescribed by white society. It also dovetailed with the age-old phenomenon of rebelling against the mores of one's parents' compromised and implicated generation.'

By 1980, the year of his first arrest, Guy had been involved for several years in student study groups, self-help groups, a township newspaper, and volunteer projects in the townships and rural areas; and, like many students, he was attracted to reading 'banned' literature. In addition to his activity in the white anti-apartheid student movement, he had also agreed to research trade unionism for the banned ANC. He had just gone to bed in the early hours of an August morning after writing an article for the *Work in Progress* journal. Suddenly, there was aggressive banging on the door. Once again the police had come to arrest him.

Initially Guy thought that his arrest was not especially serious – that he was part of a general round-up related to widespread boycotts in the local township schools, to which he was not connected. Reality sank in swiftly, he says, after he was moved to an isolated police station in the small Eastern Cape hamlet of Alexandria, where the security police, led by Alfred Oosthuizen, started serious interrogation, demanding to know when he had joined the ANC and following it up with three days of sleep deprivation, threats, assault and sweet talk. Thereafter, he was taken back to Grahamstown to write a statement, and then to prison in East London for sporadic further interrogation. He remained in solitary confinement there for another three months, before being transferred to Port Elizabeth for the formal political trial.

Guy knows he was betrayed by the notorious spy Craig Williamson, who had been involved in a chain of messages from the ANC in Botswana delivered to him by another spy, Karl Edwards. Both men testified at Guy's trial. The verdict in the Port Elizabeth court found Guy guilty of being a member of the ANC, a finding based largely on the possession and circulation of banned ANC literature. 'In fact, I wasn't a member,' Guy explains. 'At that time the ANC's internal constitutional laws even stated that white people living in South Africa couldn't be members. At any rate, in 1979–1980, I was a sympathiser, not an actual cadre. The hard evidence for the conviction was possession and distribution of ANC publications.'

In the build-up to the trial, he had been detained for three months and was moved several times – a tactic routinely used to separate detainees from their families – from Alexandria to East London to Port Elizabeth. Another four months passed after his sentencing. He was then taken to Pollsmoor Prison in Cape Town, and finally, to Pretoria.

'The first three or four days of that 1980 detention were the worst in terms of direct pressure,' he says. 'There was a combination of sleep deprivation and slapping me around. Unlike some others, I wasn't given electric shocks or made to stand on drawing pins, but the inhumane treatment was still effective.'

He was kept awake for three days and three nights, then forced to make a statement. 'You start going a bit funny after that,' he says with understatement. 'But probably even worse was to follow: solitary confinement in a tiny grey cell for twenty-three hours a day. The window is painted black, and a naked bulb is on twenty-four hours. You don't know when this ordeal will come to an end; it seems indefinite. You imagine your file is on some clerk's desk. You have no reading matter and no contact with anyone. There is only yourself and your worries.' After some time, he was allowed a Bible and sporadic visits from Jeanne, then his girlfriend – occasions that he was sure the police were bugging. To counter the eavesdropping, he would write words on the palm of his hand to show her.

It was typical of their racist thinking, Guy says, that the police assumed that he was part of a grand plan and that he was, among other things, running underground cells to recruit students for the ANC. 'They said: "Now that we have got you, we will stamp out the opposition in the Eastern Cape".' This was sincerely believed by them, Guy maintains, notwithstanding that the region had a tradition of resistance going back 150 years. 'They simply assumed that black campaigners were incapable of organising themselves and needed whites to do it for them,' he says.

'I was surprised to be arrested, in fact, because I didn't think I was really doing anything very serious or effective. It would have been nice to be a hero, but it was actually small-scale stuff – helping a bit here or there. Yet, they said in court that the things I had done were connected to hard-core recruiting.'

After Guy admitted to the police the location of a trunk containing his banned books, he was made to spend a night inventorying the contents and explaining the origin of each item. There was one piece of evidence he felt he had to get rid of for fear of incriminating an activist in East London who had given it to him. It was a photocopy of a document by the banned South African Communist Party. Surreptitiously, Guy tore it into small pieces under the desk and ate it bit by bit, spy style, while his interrogator wasn't looking – but he hadn't known that it had been copied using a particularly toxic-tasting chemical and he had to choke it down.

It's typical of Guy's nature that he remains modest about his role in the struggle. He was arrested, beaten up, kept in solitary in a tiny cell with a bucket for a toilet, and imprisoned; yet, like Zubeida and Marion, he manages to make light of it. While I am staying with the Bergers in Grahamstown, Jeanne takes me on a tour of the university's newly extended library – a project she oversaw as deputy director – and confides: 'I am so glad you are writing this book. Guy would never do it himself, yet I think the experience of talking about it could be cathartic for him.'

Theirs is clearly an extraordinary relationship. Guy and Jeanne were virtually childhood sweethearts, meeting at Rhodes, and staying true through a punishing sequence of events: arrest, detainment, torture, harassment (the police threatened to ring Jeanne and tell her that Guy had slept with another student, and they told him he would never see his father again because he would die of a heart attack during an anticipated lengthy sentence), Guy's second arrest, going into hiding and then fleeing the country, Jeanne's pregnancy, their daughter Vanessa's birth, and their eventual reuniting in London. Jeanne has maintained and developed her own career alongside his, along with raising two children, and has now relocated again with him to Paris, where he has taken up his new role as director of freedom of expression and media development at UNESCO.

Although there are plenty of women who played a dramatic part in South Africa's fight for independence, there are others who adopted quieter, less publicised, but no less important, roles, and it's clear from Guy's letters from prison that Jeanne's love helped him to stay sane. She moved to Johannesburg and took a job there in the expectation that he would serve his sentence in a Pretoria jail (in fact, he was unexpectedly sent to Cape Town for the first six months of his time). They conceived Vanessa two years after his first release in the full expectation that he would be imprisoned again, for a longer term this time.

Everyone who knows Guy knows Jeanne too, and admiration of her runs deep. She made many sacrifices, enduring loneliness while he was in prison, having a young child while her husband was on the run, and subsequently relocating to the UK in the wake of his second detention. Yet, there is another story I came across – of a contemporary of theirs, Jeannette Schoon – that haunts me, especially as I think how easily this could have been Jeanne's story. Jeannette's husband, Marius Schoon, was an associate of Guy's. They had met once in Botswana when Guy had handed over some apartheid government military documents he had come across. The security police never found out about this, and it was an act that Guy kept concealed during his detention. Marius had been imprisoned, with two others, for twelve years beginning in 1964, after the botched bombing of a radio transmitter in Joburg (which had been instigated by a police provocateur). He was released in 1976, the year of the Soweto uprising. He and fellow activist Jeannette, both of whom had been banned, left the country for Botswana. In 1984, when they were living in southern Angola with their two children, Craig Williamson, Guy's betrayer, sent a parcel bomb to Marius. Instead, it killed Jeannette and their six-year-old daughter Katryn, who were at home in their flat. Reportedly, when Williamson heard his bomb had killed them instead of Marius, he said: 'Serves them right.'[37]

'Their son Fritz, then aged three, was found wandering nearby,' says the *Independent*'s obituary for Marius, who died of cancer in 1999, having seen Williamson go free after testifying at the Truth and Reconciliation Commission.[38] Williamson murdered activist Ruth First in 1982 using the same method; and in 1988, another of his bombs blew off the arm of freedom fighter (and later Constitutional Court judge) Albie Sachs in Mozambique.

The Schoon family and Ruth First's daughters took the amnesty ruling on review, arguing that Williamson had a personal motive for the murders and had failed to make a full disclosure. He agreed to pay them and to pick up their legal costs in exchange for their dropping moves to overturn the amnesty. In 2008, he was declared bankrupt after failing to keep up the payments, and was freed from the only form of justice he had ever faced – if justice it can be called.[39] Guy tells me that he was interrogated by Williamson in 1980, and recalls a highly self-righteous character who claimed to have been appalled at once hearing Joe Slovo, Ruth First's husband, tell a political rally: 'It is not enough to die for the struggle; you have to be prepared to kill for it.' By some twist of fate, Guy and Jeanne escaped the ultimate sanction that faced so many, both in exile and within the country, although they are aware that they could have become targets.

Back in 1980, they both still had the trial to face. Guy was to be tried alongside Devan Pillay, then a student at Rhodes, now associate professor of sociology at the University of the Witwatersrand (Wits) and, like many, deeply influenced by Guy both personally and politically.

* * *

At a later date, I talk from the UK on Skype to Devan at Wits. While we speak, I am staring out into the dark and the rain of the Ashdown Forest. I ask him to think back three decades. He remembers that time with clarity and some affection, as he does Guy, who was evidently an inspiration to him.

Devan had given up a degree in architecture at the University of Cape Town to return to his hometown of East London in 1979, realising he was far more interested in politics. Here he studied politics and mathematics through UNISA and joined the South African Institute of Race Relations youth programme, Masazane.[40] There he met Bandi Biko (Steve Biko's sister), Guy and other activists, 'some of whom were underground ANC and masquerading as Black Consciousness members. And there were Marxists from Rhodes and PFP members. It was fighting times for us youngsters.'

Political activity began to pick up. In 1979, there was the boycott of Fatti's & Moni's, the pasta producer, when workers wanted union recognition, a minimum wage, shorter working hours and holiday entitlement. The following year, 1980, when Devan moved to study at Rhodes, the SASOL oil-from-coal plant was bombed on the night of 31 May. There were school boycotts across the country. There were also solidarity boycotts of Rowntree, Colgate and red meat.

Devan realised that the ANC and the Communist Party were not spent forces, but were alive and more active than the still tiny Black Consciousness Movement led by Biko. Devan became interested in the ANC and New Left Marxism through Guy, began reading banned literature and became involved in the reading programme initiated by Guy on the history of the ANC.

An ANC activist, who had been at school with his older brother, visited Devan at Rhodes in 1980 and asked him to organise a boycott of the British Lions rugby tour and participate in a boycott of the South African Indian Council[41] elections. 'I was on my way to being recruited fully,' Devan says. 'It was all very exciting and clandestine, as we were young. Guy influenced me to study sociology and journalism. I've got a lot to thank him for in that sense – the level-headed guidance he was giving at the time.'

Things were gathering momentum as the activists began to plan an exams boycott; then, in July 1980, they heard that the activist Chris Watters had been arrested – he had gone to an East London township with ANC pamphlets in the boot of his car. This event prompted the arrests of Guy and Devan. 'They tried to stitch it all together into one conspiracy,' Devan says, 'but there was only between a 20–30 per cent connection between Guy and me.'

Devan was to be in prison for eight months preceding his trial. As Marion had found, and Guy pointed out to me, there was a division in their treatment according to their skin colour. Devan was tortured; techniques included placing a wet bag over his head to suffocate him, and putting drawing pins under his feet to force him to stand on his tiptoes.

'African prisoners had even worse treatment,' says Devan. And he feels that because he and others were relatively protected by the public profile the university gave them, he wasn't subjected to the electric-shock torture that was routinely handed out to black prisoners. He also feels that class was a factor.

Like Guy, he was subjected to psychological torture, although he believes it was worse for Guy. 'They tried to trick you into giving away information, saying, "This person has already confessed", and that made you wonder about that person's loyalty. The isolation makes you feel alone, and then you strike up a bizarre relationship with these guys who are torturing you.'

Devan's mother, Daya, was a force to be reckoned with. She brought in food, not only for him, but for the policemen too. His late father had known a man called Donald Card from the Special Branch. Card was based in East London and had helped to quell the PAC uprisings in the Transkei in the 1960s. He was also a customer of the Pillay family's watchmaker and jewellery shop in East London. 'I used to work there at a young age, and I remember this guy coming in and joking with my father, and me interacting with him,' Devan recalls.

'My mother used that to try and protect me; that may have also limited the period of my torture. She got to visit me during my detention, which wasn't normally allowed. She was very outspoken, a very strong and dominant character, and she used that to great effect. But as soon as I was released and she saw me, she just burst out crying. She had kept that strength until she saw me again.'

White detainees, he says, 'came under a different type of pressure from their families, who told them they must testify, saying, "In any case, you were just getting involved as an adventure; you must get out now". For black activists, the pressure was not to testify, because they would be ostracised.

'It was part of the calculation I had to make, myself and Guy. Who was going to testify against us? If we plea-bargained, we would get a lesser sentence. If we had a trial, then we would get a higher sentence. Guy was keen on sparing people the trauma of having to testify. If you refused to testify, you went to prison.'

There would often be an anomaly in sentencing as a result: Philemon Norushe, a trade unionist, was scheduled to testify against his friend Mandla Gxanyana. He refused and was sentenced to a year in prison; Mandla himself was sentenced to only six months.

Devan took a philosophical approach to his imprisonment. 'I learned a little of meditation and yoga, both during detention and subsequently. I read a lot. I have a philosophical nature. And I read the Bible twice; it was all about struggle against the oppressor. I found that comforting to know – that God was on my side, not the oppressor's!'

A lieutenant named Van Wyk asked Devan if he wouldn't like 'a big stack of money. I thought he was trying to recruit me into the security forces and told him, "I don't like guns".' But it quickly became clear to Devan that he would be charged and that any talk of bribery or recruitment was irrelevant.

Devan points out that there were aspects of his detention that were positive. 'While awaiting trial, I could interact with Mandla [Gxanyana]. I remember at Christmas time we shared our food, we were exercising together, just the two of us. We were getting books to read. I remember one book we discussed, Émile Zola's *Germinal*. That was a deep read for us and there were a lot of issues to discuss about propagandistic writing. This hero was criticising himself and his organisation. Mandla said you don't do that.'

The experience was very stimulating. 'You felt you were doing something for the country; you were part of the struggle. I disliked being cut off from family and friends, but felt I was part of a noble cause.' He and Guy saw their lawyers together. When the magistrate came to check on them, 'I complained about the fact that white prisoners got better food. The policeman listening in to this said white people were more civilised and needed better food.'

The worst part of Devan's detention was the first two weeks, when he was interrogated in pursuit of a statement. He was taken from the prison to a police station across town to be questioned and tortured. But even here he found something he liked: 'I enjoyed the ride and I enjoyed the food. It was the food given to the police in the police hostels. One policeman was looking at me enviously and I thought he was going to take it!'

Food in the prison was bad, he says. But 'I really enjoyed the *pap* in the morning. I looked forward to it, with a bit of sugar in the middle. And I felt happy.' But the suppers were terrible. 'We were given overcooked vegetables and some strange meat; I wondered if it was stray cat.'

Contact with others during his detention was very important. 'The actual experience of interacting with the lawyers, Guy and Mandla, and the trial, seeing everybody, having the feeling that everyone was supporting us, press clippings – you did feel that you were part of something important and worthwhile. I suppose I had a bit of a buzz.'

In fact, he rather relished the trial: 'I thoroughly enjoyed the experience. Just being with Guy and out of detention. We were charged with furthering the aims of Communism and the ANC, and of being ANC members. They couldn't make the Communism charge stick and dropped it. I remember treating the whole thing lightly and irreverently – the magistrate reprimanded us for having fun and laughing, passing notes.'

Devan had written a statement, inspired by Mandela's speech at the Rivonia Trial,[42] but didn't get to testify; Guy did. 'I got really emotional when they were interrogating him and asking him personal and unfair questions.'

Devan's mother testified on his behalf as a character witness. 'The defence lawyer tried to prime her to talk about my childhood and how I experienced apartheid and the fact that my father had died. But he couldn't get her to say my suffering under apartheid resulted in my involvement in politics. He tried to get her to paint this picture of me being significantly affected by apartheid in my upbringing. She said what a good childhood I had, and she made the magistrate laugh at her account of my teenage years: "At one moment he was listening to music of Ravi Shankar, then the next, cacophonous rock music." She had the court in stitches, but she didn't say what they wanted her to say.'

The accused were then driven back to the prison. 'I remember I burst into tears in the car. I said how very frustrated I was about how they were interrogating Guy on the stand.' There was a warrant officer called Fourie whom Devan had got to know a little. 'He said, "You should have thought of that before you got involved".'

It was an oddly close relationship that Devan and many others had with their jailers and even their torturers. Fourie was divorced and would tell Devan how his ex-wife was fleecing him. Devan would ask him for a cigarette. 'Does your mother allow you to smoke?' Fourie wanted to know.

'They're all human,' Devan tells me. 'When the trial started, my friends and colleagues were astonished to see me playing cards with the policemen. I thought, I am just going to treat them as human beings.'

The system was the problem, not white people, he says. 'That was the good thing about ANC philosophy. Whites weren't our enemy. We learned from Marx that even the oppressor is a victim of the system. The cop is alienated from himself. I took this from Hindu philosophy, the books my mother was sending me – forgiveness and an understanding of why people do what they do. I humanised them.'

Another conundrum for detainees was the issue of black policemen: how could they work on the side of apartheid? Devan remembers two black policemen in particular. 'They were treated as subordinates. One said to me: "They won't let me interrogate anyone. They just send me out to get drinks. Can't I practise on you?"' The other, older policeman invited Devan to come to his farm once he was released. The policemen said that their work was just a job and they had to feed their children. Devan realised that their education had been so poor they didn't realise just how bad the apartheid system was.

He and Guy were both accused of keeping banned literature. They had each left their collection of books with the same woman, Lindy Harris, Devan's ex-girlfriend – a coincidence that may have led to the joint trial. She was arrested and interrogated, but released without charge.

Devan's banned literature included *Time Longer Than Rope* by Eddie Roux, a history of the black man's struggle for freedom in South Africa, and *Mayibuye,* a regular ANC publication whose name means 'Let it return'. Among Guy's banned publications were *No Easy Walk to Freedom* by Nelson Mandela, *Guerrilla Warfare and Marxism* edited by William Pomeroy, *The Park and Other Stories* by James Matthews, *Forced Landing* edited by Mothobi Mutloatse, *African Patriots: The Story of the African National Congress* by Mary Benson, *The Barrel of a Gun: Political Power in Africa and the Coup d'État* by Ruth First, *Pedagogy of the Oppressed* by Paolo Freire, *Staffrider* literary magazine, the *South African Labour Bulletin* and the journal *Work in Progress*.

* * *

Back in Grahamstown, Guy recalls for me the final day of the trial.

'There was the question of how we'd end it, Devan and me. He'd been badly tortured but he was much more psychologically sound than I was. We weren't going to take the sentence lying down.

'We decided to wait for the magistrate to have left the courtroom. We didn't want to get another charge for contempt of court. We put our fists in the air and turned round to the spectators, but we decided we wouldn't chant. Neither of us were members of the ANC, even though we were found guilty of being members. We wanted to show we were defiant but that we weren't hard-core members.'

What happened after?

'We were taken down.'

How did that feel?

'I don't think I was sure of what sentence to expect. At that point, I was so exhausted by the proceedings, it was good to have a resolution. Devan was happy to stand for quite a long time with his fist in the air, but I thought we should go. We'd made our point.'

They had decided to show in court that they were well-meaning people. 'In fact, when he interrogated me during the detention period, Williamson said we were what Lenin called "the blind idiots". We were being used by evil people and had naively gone along with it. Not that we took that line. We took full responsibility for our actions and had no remorse. I think some of the police were still pissed off that we were uncowed after we'd received our sentence. They were glaring at us for giving the salute. So I said goodbye to Devan and I didn't see him again for two years because we were sent to different prisons.

'In the trial, besides my giving my statement, they also had to try to prove a case. Ever since I'd been at Rhodes, I'd been doing these study groups. We were reading about the socio-political economy of South Africa. We wanted to work these things out. You learned at university that it wasn't just a race issue. It was also a class issue, about a system that delivered cheap labour at huge human cost.

'We hated such a hurtful reality and were searching for knowledge about how to change it. The police regarded the study groups as cells recruiting students into more serious activity, but I wasn't in that league at all. But in order to make it seem more sinister than it was, they brought in a professor of politics from the then Rand Afrikaans University [now the University of Johannesburg], Stoffel van der Merwe.

'He'd been an expert witness several times over. He said there was a very typical pattern among these Communists – that they have these groups and that's how they indoctrinate young people. The small-town magistrate was very impressed. He had police spy Karl Edwards as a witness, then Craig Williamson as a witness and then this professor as a witness. He'd likely never had a case that had been so exciting and dramatic.

'He was definitely inclined to believe we had been up to the worst. We were pretty low-key, actually. Meanwhile, that same professor who was a state witness eventually became responsible for constitutional development in the cabinet of President F.W. de Klerk in the 1990s. When I came back from exile and I was editor of the *South* newspaper, I thought I would interview him. At the last minute he cancelled, so I asked his assistant if we could do it telephonically and this was agreed.

'I introduced myself as the *South* editor and he asked me what questions I wanted to put to him. I said, "I'm not sure if you remember me." He said my name sounded familiar. So I told him that he had given evidence against me at my trial and that I'd been sent to prison for two years. There was just silence at the other end of the phone. I really enjoyed that. He said, "It's coming back to me." I asked him if he could explain his turnabout: "In 1980, you were helping to put the ANC and their sympathisers in prison, but now you're in government and working a settlement with them. What explains your change of attitude?" He hummed and hawed. We published the story under the headline, "Berger interviews the man who sent him to jail".'

* * *

For his part, Devan was shocked at his sentence. A policeman had told his mother that he would get a year; he was sentenced to two. Someone gave him a copy of: *Gold and Workers: A People's History of South Africa* by Luli Callinicos. Clutching it in his hand, he went downstairs into the cell full of common-law prisoners. 'I was dressed in my smart suit – the only suit I had ever possessed. They thought I was a lawyer, then realised I was a political prisoner. Normally I would have been horrified to be with them, but here they were looking up to me.'

The same was true of his sentence in Leeuwkop Prison, Bryanston. He was reunited with Mandla Gxanyana and Philemon Norushe. They exercised together and sang liberation songs. 'I do remember very vividly that when we first got into prison, we heard the prisoners singing pop songs. Shortly after that, they were singing political songs.' Devan made sure that he engaged with both the common-law prisoners and the white warders: 'They were also working-class and oppressed by the system.'

He had hoped to be transferred to Robben Island,[43] as Leeuwkop was seen as a transit point. When he wasn't, 'it was a big disappointment, partly because we had heard that they had a much better library, but also because it would be an opportunity to meet these famous prisoners. Mandela was the most famous, although we weren't particularly enamoured with him at the time. He was seen as a moderate nationalist, but not a Marxist revolutionary. None of us believed in the Freedom Charter. We were all interested in a socialist revolution.'

Devan carried on doing yoga every day, using a book by Winnie Young that Guy had given him, and studying through UNISA. A prison warder came to congratulate him when he received a good mark. When his lawyer came to tell him his sentence had been cut in half, he told her: 'But I have to finish my studies first – this is such a great place to study!'

I ask him whether it was all worth it. 'I remember it with great pride,' he replies, 'even though I'm very critical of the ANC at the moment. It was a very valuable and noble experience – a character-building experience. We had few illusions about the ANC, even at that time. That critical Marxist perspective made us aware that the ANC was a nationalist organisation.

'We looked at what happened in other colonised countries and how they hijacked the class struggle and how the elite were advanced. We were hoping to prevent that from happening. What we didn't expect was that they got that negotiated settlement so quickly.

'But now a new working-class party is being discussed with great intensity; hopefully it will bear fruit, and either these pressures from the left towards the ANC or from the right will cause it to revitalise and come back to its better values, or a new force will emerge. This is part of our critique. This is where I differ from some friends who don't acknowledge some problems have happened. We have a great health minister, some good things happening, amid other things we don't like – corruption, and the inability to address inequality and unemployment.'

The biggest contribution of Mandela, he says, 'is what he represents on a human level, "being the change you want to see", as Gandhi said. He brought us to settlement – to exchange political power for retention of the economic elite. His passing has allowed us to have a rich national debate around his legacy. It has personal qualities that we should dwell on.'

However, says Devan, 'Mandela gave away too much. There was a fake reconciliation without social justice.'

* * *

Guy began his sentence in Port Elizabeth, where he was kept in solitary confinement, and his spirits dropped very low. He had hoped to be moved to Pretoria so that his parents and Jeanne could visit him, but was instead moved to Pollsmoor in Cape Town, where Mandela would be held in the years prior to his release in 1990. He was later moved to Pretoria, where he had the company of a handful of other white political prisoners. He was happier there.

His letters at this time, mostly to Jeanne, were generous, loving and often sharply self-critical. What is also notable is his often playful mood and the humour that shines through his writing. Initially, he was allowed only one letter a month; any extra letters were held back from him. The text was often censored. He had experienced this earlier during his trial, when he had been refused permission to send Jeanne a letter containing a rather sweet picture he had drawn of two cats – one black, one white – with their tails entwined. 'They thought it was a subversive political message,' Guy explained.

On the eve of his sentencing, Guy wrote a letter addressed, 'Dear friends', wishing to communicate with all those who had supported him. He was aware that once he was convicted, both letters and visits would be restricted. 'I mean this letter as an embrace,' he wrote, and confided his concern at the distance that might grow over one, two or three years. The letter continued:

> In the meantime, I want to ask you not to worry about me. I know I will cope with a jail sentence. Sometimes when I look for the whys and wherefores, I feel I am on the absurd side of Alice's looking glass. Moreover, since I do not feel I've really done anything significant, I do not feel like a martyr. But I cope by remembering that many people arbitrarily suffer through circumstances beyond their control. I remember specifically people who are imprisoned for pass laws and Group Areas[44] infringements.

The letter finished thus:

> I know that no matter whether I and others are removed from society, people remain who, in their own individual ways, will work towards reducing poverty and creating a happier and more democratic society. It is with this certain knowledge that I know I shall live the future years immune to feelings of despondency, dejection and frustration.

In fact, although his naturally ebullient nature was to help him get through his time in prison, there were factors that made it difficult for him to stay buoyant. First, there were the months he had to spend in Port Elizabeth and then Pollsmoor. He felt keenly the absence of Jeanne and he missed his parents' home, to which she was a frequent visitor. He wrote:

> I really envy you – or not really I suppose, anyway I think of you – being at 103. It is really nice in summer – swims, lovely long and beautiful evenings, greenness, shade, fruit trees, thick green veld.

But beyond the nostalgia for times past and the affection for his family, what shines through the letters is his love for Jeanne. In a letter dated 15 January 1981, while awaiting trial, Guy revealed his concern at the news that additional charges would be brought against him, including one with a minimum five-year sentence (which did not materialise):

> You said in your letter ... that I really was 'so brave and strong. Yes, I do think you are strong to cope with everything you've been through and are experiencing.' I think you know that I barely coped, and in fact I was quite a wreck until recently when I have been slowly building myself again. I think you also know that it was not so much 'bravery or strength' that kept me going when I was at my lowest, but my knowledge of how much my life meant to you ... the knowledge of your love for me gives me my most important reason for existing.

He also declared his intention to evaluate the actions that had landed him in prison:

> I now want to help myself emotionally by looking at the good points. I now want to look for things where I can say with surety, 'There, I have nothing to regret. There I did what was right and good. There – even if some of my motive was egoism – there were also the good motives of compassion and longing for fairness in the world.'

What helped him throughout his sentence was playing the recorder, practising yoga, running – and studying. He completed an honours degree through UNISA and began an MA thesis (which was later converted to a PhD dissertation, published by Cambridge University Press some ten years later).

'When I was on trial, they allowed me to get in an old apple-carton of papers and photocopies that I had and, notes on my MA thesis, which was on rural development projects in the Ciskei region. I was allowed to keep that all the way through my sentence, surprisingly. In the prison, there were a lot of other photocopied articles and books people had collected over the years. Over twenty years of political imprisonment, people had built up libraries. The readings were very eclectic, but it was refreshing to engage with the range of materials.'

After his release in 1983, he continued sporadic work on his dissertation, giving it a final push in 1985 while hiding during the then State of Emergency. In the rush to leave for exile in the UK, he left a slightly earlier version with a friend to print, bind and submit. It was rejected and he had to rework it. 'So for ten years I had this postgraduate study hanging over me like the proverbial millstone. But anyway, I got it in the end … I just wanted to finish it. I didn't necessarily see myself as having an academic career. I just wanted to get it done, hopefully as a useful contribution to scholarship.'

He was released from prison in 1983. 'I thought Jeanne and I would have to leave the country, so we got married very quickly as we thought it would be easier to live abroad that way. If you're really high profile, then it makes sense to stay and be a martyr, but I thought I could be more effective if I left. What's the point of being a martyr if nobody knows about you? I thought I could do more from abroad.'

But he was soon arrested again, after helping to produce leaflets for the United Democratic Front (UDF),[45] calling for a stayaway in 1984. He was in detention for some two weeks, then released.

'There was so much resistance in the townships that the government couldn't cope with just having the police, so they sent in the army. The army went into the townships in the Vaal region and there was a huge stayaway. It went on for about three or four days. That's when the security police decided to crack down. It was clear that you could send the army in, but that doesn't stop a stayaway – and a stayaway disrupts the economy.'

Guy and Jeanne were staying in Berea in Joburg at the time. 'The police came knocking at the door and, lo and behold, it was Oosthuizen again. He knew that he had quite a lot of power to intimidate me from the previous time. He said: "Why are you still bringing trouble on yourself and others by being involved in this stuff? Now we're going to search your books."

'I was a bit more cocky then. I said: "You can search them, but you've searched them before." I came out of prison more hardened. When you've been at a low point, when you put yourself together again and other people help you, you become more resilient.'

The police did a search, but this time they did not find a cache of banned publications. Nonetheless, Guy was arrested and taken to John Vorster Square.

'We were walking up the stairs and this very aggressive cop came up and he said: "*Wie's jy?* [Who are you?]" I said, "I'm Guy Berger", and he said, "You're a fucking Communist", and shoved me down the stairs. I thought, I hadn't even gotten into the offices and they were behaving like thugs. When I got upstairs, I said that I wanted to lay a charge of assault against this guy.

69

'At that point, because of the pressures of the international community and the internal resistance, magistrates had to come and check that detainees weren't being tortured. So the magistrate came and I said I wanted to lay this charge. He said there were no witnesses and they couldn't prosecute him and I had no medical report, and so on.

'But by lodging a complaint I sent out a signal to them that I was not going to be a pushover. I thought to myself that I was going to start laying a trail, because if I was going to end up making a statement about being involved in the stayaway pamphlets, I could say that the statement wasn't made voluntarily, because I would have this track record of lodging complaints, and, somewhere along the line, it would be hard to cover all that stuff up.

'That was my strategy, so every time they were brutal or threatened brutality, I would lay a charge. I was documenting it all. I was completely denying having any involvement in the stayaway or the propaganda planning the stayaway.

'The police brought in this colleague of mine, Obed Bapela, who, incidentally, twenty-five years later became deputy minister in the Department of Communications. They'd already beaten him up very badly and they said, "If you don't talk, we're going to beat him up more".

'Then they said that they'd had him in detention for two weeks and he hadn't asked for a toothbrush, which "just shows what kind of backward people they are". It was crazy.

'At one point they brought in another guy who had also been badly beaten, and they said that he had confessed that I was involved and had done a leaflet with him. It was true. I *had* done a leaflet with this guy. His name was Oupa Monareng.[46]

'But having been in prison the first time, I had met fellow prisoners who had never seen their children growing up. Like fellow prisoner David Rabkin, who later died in Angola. It was very painful, because he would see his kids through glass. He could never hug them. Jeanne was pregnant. I just thought, Screw this; I really am not going back to prison if I can help it. I wanted to be released and see my child born.

University days, driving home to Johannesburg: L to R: Jannie Roux, Leslie Cooper, Janet Shapiro, Guy and Jeanne.

Graduation day at Rhodes: Guy with fellow student activists Chris Watters (left, later detained with him) and Sue Myrdal (right).

*The image of these black and white cats with their tails intertwined was
enough to stop Guy's letter reaching Jeanne: the prison governor thought it
was an anti-apartheid image.*

*Jeanne and Guy outside court in Port Elizabeth during his trial in 1981, the
relief at the end of his detention clear on their faces.*

Guy Berger, then head of the School of Journalism and Media Studies at Rhodes University, in one of the lecture halls.

Jeanne and Guy Berger in Paris, where he is now Director of Freedom of Expression and Media Development for UNESCO.

Marion Sparg on her release in 1991, photographed by Karen Hurt for SPEAK magazine.

Jacaranda season: Joy, Marion and Michelle in their garden at home.

Marion with her daughters Michelle (left) and Joy (middle) doing homework in their home. in Joburg.

Then president Thabo Mbeki with Marion and her elder daughter Michelle at Walter Sisulu's 90th birthday party, 18 May 2002.

Janice and Marion at lunch with the family: picture taken by Michelle, Marion's daughter.

Zubeida and her daughter Ruschka, now a graduate of the University of Cape Town, in the garden of their home.

Zubeida with her neighbour and close childhood friend Evelyn (Evie) Samuels, circa 1966.

Zubeida at court in 1980, facing charges of possessing three banned books.

Dark days: Zubeida back at home in 1987 when her husband Jonny had been forced into hiding.

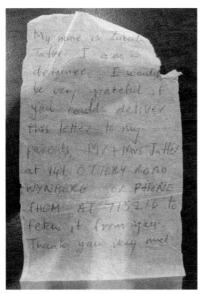

Letters from prison: A note that Zubeida wrote to accompany one of the letters she wrote on toilet paper in prison, hoping someone would post or deliver it to her family.

Cuttings from the Cape Times *about Zubeida's arrest and detention.*

A remarkable woman: Mrs Raghmat Jaffer, Zubeida's mother, on the eve of her 85th birthday.

'In fact, we decided to have a child because there was a strong chance I would be arrested again, and if I was I might be in for a long time. It wasn't an ideal time to start thinking about a child, but it was a kind of insurance. Anyway, when I was in detention for the second time, I was very resilient.

'So they were beating up this guy Oupa Monareng; he had cuts on his face and so on. They were saying he'd confessed my involvement. He was being humiliated in front of me. They were saying he'd implicated me so I might as well 'fess up, but I said no, I wouldn't. I said maybe he was just a guy who has problems with whites and maybe he was just trying to get his revenge on me because I'm white. I made a completely preposterous statement.

'After that, Oosthuizen came in. They knew I was lying but they couldn't torture me. Oosthuizen was telling me to get it over and done with. I was still scared of him. He had messed me around emotionally the first time with his combination of blackmail and bullying. He said I had to make a statement, so I did. But I jumbled the statement. I had this thought that if I was called into court on the back of the statement, I could say it wasn't really me.

'They didn't really understand media production. So in explaining how I had made this leaflet, I used broken English and they just transcribed it. I said, "I cutted the bromide", so they wrote, "I cutted the bromide". That's not how I talk. And in fact, the way I'd outlined media production, it really didn't make sense at all. What was the bromide used for? Indirectly, for making the printing plates. You first had to make a negative out of it, but I left out this stage of production in the statement.

'There was actually a lot of international protest at the time. Even [US president] Ronald Reagan was saying they should release us. So they did. There were about twelve people who were arrested in connection with the stayaway. After about two weeks, they charged three guys, including Monareng. Then they immediately gave them bail, but the court case fell away because they skipped the country.

There were no more accused, so I never had to go to court and be a state witness. If I had had to, I would have said my statement had been forced out of me, and if push came to shove, I would have refused to testify – and then I would have been facing five years in prison anyway. It wasn't a nice position to be in.'

So you went about it all in a much more sophisticated way. You knew how to use the system.

'Yes. I was twenty-eight, as opposed to twenty-four, and four years makes a big difference, especially seeing as I'd been through it before. The first time I'd been detained, I'd heard that there was this thing of "good cop, bad cop". So I was looking out for that, but what I wasn't looking out for was Oosthuizen acting both roles. You couldn't predict what he was going to do. It was very disruptive for me in my first detention experience.

'Sometimes he would be very charming and friendly and talk to you as if he wasn't going to get heavy with you, and then there were times he would get very rough with you and that would take you by surprise. The person whom you thought was OK would then come out and say something like, "You won't see your father for fifteen years". The second time round, I knew that one cop could combine those two roles.'

So what happened? Did Oosthuizen get worse and worse?

'He was then too much of a big fish in the system to be doing the interrogation himself. He would just come and intervene and use his influence and reputation to tilt the balance. He was a very sophisticated interrogator. What's interesting is that the others were amateurs. You could bullshit them. He was far more of a pro.'

Alfred Oosthuizen had been head of the Security Branch in the 1970s and 1980s; he had subsequently been posted to Johannesburg. Later, he was head of the Security Branch intelligence section in charge of killings of ANC operatives in and out of the country; he gave chilling evidence at the Truth and Reconciliation Commission hearings, where he and others asked for amnesty.

Not all interrogators had the same skills. During Guy's first detention back in 1980, a second interrogator, Lieutenant Van Wyk, the same man who had interrogated Devan Pillay, 'was not nearly as fluent in English as Oosthuizen and was not nearly as clever. He didn't have the interrogation techniques of Oosthuizen. It was just the usual police brutality. Anyway, one day Oosthuizen said: "Today, you're really going to *kak* off."[47] I could see what was coming – and what was coming actually was that Craig Williamson was going to interrogate me. He was recently back in South Africa after living in Switzerland and had been exposed as a police agent, working directly with the police.

'In fact, the *Sunday Times* had this front-page photo, which had appeared even before I was detained. The caption said "Our man in Moscow", with a picture of Williamson standing in Red Square. Apparently, he just went as a tourist. But the thing was that he had infiltrated this network, him and Karl Edwards [another spy]. So Lieutenant Van Wyk said I was going to be in trouble now "because Williamson is going to interrogate you". Williamson had this huge reputation as a South African "superspy", as the *Sunday Times* had called him.

'So they took me into this office in the security police headquarters, and there was this guy standing with his back to me, looking out of the window. His hands were behind his back. He turned around very majestically. I said something like "Good morning, Captain Williamson". He gave the impression he hadn't even heard me. He said, "Do you *know* who I am?" He was really living it up. He had such a high opinion of himself!

'And then he started interrogating me. He might have been a good spy, but he was useless at interrogating. The one mistake he made was that he talked more about himself than he was asking me questions. In the same way as Karl Edwards fainted in court. It was psychological stress for these guys.

'Here I was, a well-meaning young person, sickened at apartheid, but they had played a role in getting me involved and now they had to come face to face with the damage they'd caused. At my trial Edwards fainted. He couldn't take the stress of seeing me there. Williamson started saying to me: "I know you from the student movement, of course. I can see you're a decent guy. But I don't know why you want to support these guys".

'He was trying to justify himself. He even got to the point where he said he was against the ANC because they were Communists and terrorists, but he said he was still working through the religion issue. He wasn't completely sure if he believed in God yet.

'This was bizarre. He was giving his personal justification to me. I was sitting there thinking, Thank God he's rabbiting on, because the more he talks, the less I have to. He was showing weakness. He was inexperienced, but it was pathetic. He was kind of a hero for the South African police, but he was losing respect very fast among those diehard, hands-on, cold-faced interrogators who had been around.'

How did your parents react to your political activities?

'When I was arrested in 1980, they were really shocked,' Guy says. But during his time in detention and then in prison, his mother was a whirlwind of activity. Guy still has many of her letters. She was demanding and forthright, and no doubt a thorn in the side of the prison authorities. Nevertheless, when she saw him on his release, she said to Guy, 'I want to ask you a really serious question. Do you *really* believe in one person, one vote?'

He laughs out loud telling me this story, saying, 'At the time, I was really a socialist!'

When the police came a third time for Guy, during 1985, he realised his time was up. After three months in hiding, during a State of Emergency when scores of his colleagues were detained, he left for exile. The destination was London, where he worked for Afravision, a venture set up with two other Rhodes graduates: his best friend Tony Pinchuck, and his friend and former housemate Barbara McCrea. They sold video news footage from South Africa largely taken by the Video News Service (VNS) collective of Brian Tilley – another

74

member of the class of '79 – and his colleagues, Lawrence Dworkin and Mokoenyana Molete.

* * *

Tony and Guy were inseparable. They had met at Rhodes; Tony's family moved there when his father, Isidore Pinchuck, was invited to create a School of Translation at the university in 1975. I know Tony too, although I only met him properly years later in the UK, when he and Barbara McCrea began a relationship. They married in our garden in Sussex in 1984 in a Unitarian ceremony, and are co-authors of the *Rough Guides* to South Africa, Zimbabwe and Cape Town. They have a son, Gabriel, and are now divorced.

I speak with Tony, then art director at *Noseweek,* the Cape Town–based investigative magazine, about how he and Guy had met. I had pictured them as childhood friends.

Tony tells me: 'We met in the politics class – Nancy Charton's class. We had tutorials together. Nancy thought a lot of Guy. She thought he was the brightest student she had ever had.

'She wasn't on Guy's wavelength politically. But she had this amazing ability to appreciate him, despite the fact that his ideas were completely different. Often, I think, she didn't understand what he was on about. He got phenomenally high marks for these incredibly long essays he would write.'

How did you connect?

'There was just something there. One of those intangible, chemical things.'

'Guy reminds me of you,' I tell Tony. He does; they could be brothers. They have the same smile – it's uncanny.

What was Guy like when you first met him? Presumably he was a political being even then.

'He was always an independent thinker. He read a lot. I'm not sure where the interest in Marxism came from. There was stuff we would

75

talk about and write about. I remember sitting at my parents' dining room table and writing our essays. There were these piles of books and we just wrote and wrote and wrote. But Guy wrote twice as much as I did. One was about a seventy-page essay; I'm not kidding. It went on and on. No wonder he ended up with a PhD.'

How soon did you sense Guy was politically involved?

'He was always involved. He was much more engaged than I ever was. I was a commentator, a cartoonist. He was more of a figure. He was charismatic. At some point we worked out how to form societies on campus and how to use them to promote political ideas. We formed a psychology society and there was an organisation called Delta[48] that Guy basically took control of. I think it became significant.'

Tony tells me he was also questioned by Guy's mother about his political beliefs. 'I went to stay with Guy in Joburg. His mum came to me and asked why Guy did the stuff he did. She understood him wanting to help black people, but she didn't know why he did what he did. She didn't know what he was about at all. I sidestepped it. I sensed there was no way to engage with this properly.'

Tony graduated in 1978 with a psychology degree and arrived in London in 1979 as a political refugee. He had refused to do national service and contacted the anti-apartheid movement in the form of the Committee on South African War Resistance (COSAWR), which provided refuge for war resisters looking for political asylum. Based in London and Amsterdam, COSAWR also worked with European anti-apartheid movements to impose sanctions on the anti-apartheid regime.[49]

'I'd actually been over the year before and met up with one of the guys. I'd met them under a *nom de guerre*. I was very nervous. I didn't know if I was going to stay in South Africa.

'I drew cartoons for *Resister*, a publication put together by war resisters living in London and edited by Gavin Cawthra. In fact, when my brother was doing his national service in the army, he and the others were shown the "horrible stuff that the Communists were producing in London", and he saw a cartoon and recognised it as mine.'

Jeanne said to me that Guy actually cried when you went away.

'We have this funny relationship because we don't talk to each other for months, but it's still the same when we do. It was actually years that I didn't talk to him because he was in jail, with no means of communication.'

I remember how South Africans met. They would circle around each other like dogs in a park, wondering which one was a spy.

'That was the pernicious thing. You were never quite sure who was a spy.

'When Guy was arrested – he was arrested twice, this must have been the first time – I was living in Tottenham. I was sharing a house with a British guy. I was stunned. I think I actually wept. The other guy asked if I was OK, and I got the sense he didn't understand what it really meant.

'The next thing was that Guy phoned me in September 1984. He didn't come to our wedding. I don't think I knew he'd been released. My memory of it is that the phone rang and it was Guy. He said he thought he was going to get arrested again.'

You told me he arrived with this heavy suitcase and a pillow and books inside. Did you ask him about it?

'No, I don't think I did. I felt it was perhaps because the pillow represented home and comfort; he had only just been released.

'Barbara and I were there, meditating. The phone rang and I heard it, but left it to the answering machine to take a message. Eventually Guy went off to the IDAF [International Defence and Aid Fund].[50] He then had to track us down at the new office, which I think was in Islington. He'd been traipsing all over the place. He'd arrived in this strange city. I don't think he'd been before. He stayed with us. Then Jeanne came over with the girls. Guy was doing all sorts of stuff. He distributed the *Weekly Mail*. He was very energetic. He would personally drop off the newspaper at various houses. He was involved in Afravision. It started off as me and Barbara and him, then mainly him and Barbara. They were the London presence.

'Then he ended up at the *Morning Star*, on the foreign news desk. It sounds very grand, but it was actually quite small. There were two of them – him and Roger Trask, a Brit. They worked together for years. I just think it was interesting that when he was at the *Morning Star* that was when the Eastern Bloc collapsed. Guy was starting to wake up to the fact that the whole thing sucked. There were quite interesting tensions at the paper. I worked there for a bit, with Guy.

'It was interesting, just thinking about how he built himself up from scratch again. He's very motivated. I remember how full of dog shit London used to be, and Guy saying that his mum and dad had come to stay and they had asked him how he could live somewhere with so much dog shit around. And he said, "I don't look at the streets, I look at the sky." I thought that was nice.'

* * *

Once Mandela was released in 1990, Guy, Jeanne and their daughters, Vanessa and Alexia, returned to South Africa. Guy worked for *South*, an offshoot of the *Weekly Mail,* before returning to his alma mater as head of the School of Journalism. Jeanne became a senior librarian at Rhodes, and later deputy chief librarian. Both daughters followed Guy on the journalism degree – one studied graphic design and the other photography.

Guy also ran Highway Africa, the largest annual gathering of African journalists in the world, where the subject of press freedom is high on the agenda, and where the fact that South Africa is way ahead of many other countries didn't escape him. In 2011, he and Jeanne left Rhodes, and he took a job as director of freedom of expression and media development at UNESCO in Paris – a two-year position that was renewed for another two years at the end of 2013.

When I first stayed with Guy and Jeanne in 2010, Jeanne had been busy with the launch of the new library, and she and I did not succeed in sitting down to talk together. Three years later, we speak by telephone: she is in her flat in the *16th arrondissement* in Paris, where she and Guy have lived for two years. Guy is in Canada, and on his return they are heading for a conference in Bali, then to Cape Town for Christmas, where they have just bought a house. She gave up her job to accompany Guy to his new position. 'I initially thought I was not ready to give up work,' she says, 'but it has been wonderful to have time to myself. I miss my colleagues and, initially, I battled a bit with my identity. But I am very comfortable with myself at the moment.'

The peace and elegance of the *16th arrondissement* is a far cry from the political turmoil of South Africa in the late 1970s. Jeanne met Guy at a student party, when they were both nineteen, and what she describes as 'infatuation, followed by love' followed.

By August 1980, when he was detained, 'we had been together for quite a while. We'd been through our ups and downs, break-ups and make-ups, during our student years. I had spent a year in East London in 1979 teaching and then went back to Grahamstown to study librarianship. We had a big commitment to each other, but it was still a reasonably immature relationship. Then when he was detained, they used his relationship with me to psychologically torture him. It was a very tough thing for him. He had been a little bit unfaithful to me while I was in East London, and they were threatening him with telling me.

'The first time I was able to see him was probably about a month after he was detained. He just broke down and told me about it. Although it was really tough, it just brought us together more in a way. To secure my visits with him, we said we were engaged, though we weren't formally engaged. At some point we asked if we could get married; they said no.'

Jeanne admits she wasn't naturally political, but it didn't take long for Guy's views to influence her. 'I wasn't politically active when I met Guy, and I suppose I slowly changed. I had some political awareness. I was against apartheid – his views were not contrary to what I believed in.'

Quite quickly, though, she was being exposed to a far more political world. 'I had been a *joller* [partygoer] at Rhodes; he was very different to my other friends. I was politicised far more through meeting Guy. I wasn't studying politics – I did a degree in psychology and zoology.

'It was 1977 when I was exposed to the more serious side of politics – when Biko died. We were giving a lift to someone who was organising Biko's funeral when we were stopped by the police – he was hiding in the car. This was about a year after I had initially met Guy.' By this time Guy and a few others had started the Delta organisation, and in 1978 Jeanne started going to the Thornhill resettlement camp,[51] where she ran sewing groups.

Guy's arrest was a blur, she says. It happened in the early hours of a morning in August 1980. 'I remember being really shocked. They got me in a few days later, into the office above the OK Bazaars in town, and questioned me for a couple of hours. I didn't know anything about what he was doing. I knew he was going to Botswana and seeing Pete Richer [a deported former Rhodes University student]. He hadn't told me where the banned books were. I was a bit useless to them.'

What was your lowest point?

'Well, I think the initial shock, and then the initial period when I didn't know where he was. I had no clue what was happening and I was very frightened by it all, just the uncertainty about what was going to happen, and the constant stress.' It was a week or two before she knew where he was being held – first in Alexandria police station, then in East London.

Deaths in police custody were rife during these years. With the power given to them by the laws governing detention without trial, the police had no obligation to tell relatives where prisoners were being held or how long they were likely to remain in custody.

'In 1978, we had stayed on Allendale Farm outside Grahamstown for the second half of the year. The students who had stayed there before us were into drugs. There was a raid on the farm and Guy said it was a pretext – that they were security police, not drugs police.'

But there was a lot of support and aid for detainees' families, and throughout Guy's detention, trial and imprisonment, Jeanne found invaluable help from the Detainees' Parents Support Committee, where 'Sheila Suttner, mother of Raymond Suttner [an ANC activist who suffered eleven years of imprisonment and house arrest], was incredibly supportive'. The organisation played an important role for families of detainees: meeting other people who had family members in prison or who were detained, and who were going through similar stresses, was invaluable. 'I think to know one wasn't alone was very important,' says Jeanne.

She also joined the Johannesburg Democratic Action Committee (JODAC), which was part of the UDF. 'I was pretty politicised at that stage, and I was mixing with a lot of people who were in the same league, so it was a supportive environment.' The workplace could also be helpful during this time of high detention numbers. When she was working for the Johannesburg Public Library, she had no trouble being granted time off to visit Guy in prison.

Do you think Guy's detention drew you closer together?

'Yes. I often think about what would have happened to our relationship if that hadn't happened. It drew us closer and made us realise we did want to be together. There's no doubt in my mind that I wanted to wait for Guy. I did see a couple of other guys and went out, but I knew in my mind that Guy was the one for me.

'Once he was put on trial, oddly, things became easier. I kept a clip from the *Eastern Province Herald* – a photo of us; we look so happy. The picture was taken during the trial but we look like we were getting married!

'There was terrible stress, but there was also the joy of seeing him, and we were able to have physical contact. There was a weird, contradictory set of emotions. And there was a sense of relief, at the end of the trial, that there was some closure.'

Once Guy had been sentenced (to seven years, three suspended – so effectively four years, reduced to two on appeal), an end was in sight. 'Other people were detained for years – there was no end to it,' Jeanne says. And visiting him in prison meant she was dealing with the prison bureaucracy and not the police, which was marginally better.

'It was still stressful having him inside. As much as I looked forward to seeing him in prison, I can still remember sitting there on one side of the glass and being watched over – it was pretty unpleasant. And I remember being in Pretoria prison, going along the corridors, with the keys clanging.

'I think the one time I have seen Guy depressed is when we first went to England. It was a tough year, being yanked away from a world that he had been so politically involved in. The ANC advised him to be in England, out of the whole South African situation.'

But that didn't happen straightaway. When Guy came out of prison, he and Jeanne thought he would have to leave the country. But then he went to work for a community media centre producing resistance media, and was again politically involved.

The second detention was in November 1984, when Guy was held for about two weeks. Jeanne was pregnant at the time. Then, not long after the birth of her first daughter (Vanessa), the July 1985 State of Emergency was declared on the night of Guy's birthday.

'We were living in Crown Mines in Berea, a lefty kind of place, old mine houses with alternative people living there. We had been there for six months. We had gone to the drive-in with Vanessa to see a James Bond film. Then on the way back, we bought a *Sunday Times*, which said the police may come and round people up on the first night.' So Guy left to stay with people they knew.

The police came at 4am. Jeanne was at home on her own with Vanessa. 'They locked my phone and hid the key so I couldn't ring out, turned the place upside down and then left. It was a freezing-cold night; I couldn't get warm. It's a terrifying, vivid memory, of me on my own with Vanessa.'

In the weeks to come, 'the police would pop round and say, "Have you seen Guy? When you see him, tell him we want to ask him a few questions."'

If they had wanted to find Guy, she says, they could have done so. 'For the police, the main thing was to get people out of the way and not politically involved. They knew I was seeing him. For them, the main thing was that he was lying low. If they really had wanted to track him down, they could have. He grew a moustache as a disguise – it looked awful! We met at our neighbours' place and I was so relieved he had stayed away that night. Then we went to stay with a friend whose uncle had a house in Springs. Later we went to Salt Rock, where Guy's parents had a home.'

While in hiding, Guy stayed with friends in Brixton, Johannesburg. 'They had a child who was slow in walking. Guy got her to walk – she was called Amelia.

'Then, when we came back to Joburg, he left South Africa. I was too terrified to go to the airport with his parents – they could have stopped him at the airport. He decided to go to London, as the ANC wanted him there. There was a big South African community in London and he had been given asylum.'

Guy left in September, and Jeanne and Vanessa followed him two months later. 'I had to pack up the house. We had to get rid of a lot of stuff – it went to a Black Sash[52] fete. I had to make the choices as to what we kept, and we still joke about it sometimes when he asks where a particular album is.'

When Jeanne arrived in London, she faced the problems encountered by many immigrants. 'I had bought a little tracksuit for Vanessa and thought she would be warm enough in that. I soon realised this is a whole different climate.' Other South Africans helped out. 'A woman in the ANC gave me a whole lot of clothes including a snowsuit.' Eager to get Vanessa out to the park, Jeanne would get her all dressed up only to find – like all mothers in cold climates – that the baby's nappy needed changing and that she would have to undress her and start again.

'It was desperately cold. We stayed in the downstairs section of the house; there was no central heating. There were gas fires in the bedrooms and our friends put a tiny electric heater in the bathroom for us. It was too cold even to bath Vanessa.'

She remembers one particular incident. 'One horrendous evening, I had been feeding Vanessa, lying on the bed. Then I put her in her cot and left the room. I heard a crash and ran back to the room. Part of the ceiling had fallen onto the bed where I had been feeding her fifteen minutes before.' Nevertheless, they were happy living in Brixton, London, sharing the house with friends who were very supportive.

After a year, they moved to Tottenham, to the house of a South African woman who had moved to Lesotho. The house had central heating and it was much closer to the IDAF in Islington, where Jeanne worked as a librarian, running the resource centre and news-cuttings collection. The IDAF carried out research and published books, and raised funds to support prisoners and their families. 'It was a great organisation to work for, linked with the anti-apartheid movement,' Jeanne says.

She took a year off when Alexia was born, and then relied on child-minders when she returned to work. 'In retrospect, sometimes I think, Did we do the right thing? The child-minder used a playpen when she needed to do things, and as the children got a bit older, she plonked them in front of the TV. It was probably not the best, but they were safe.'

The challenges of life in Britain were different, she points out. 'When we were in Brixton and we first used a child-minder, I used to get a bus to take Vanessa there, than take a bus back and get on the Underground.' Coming from a reasonably comfortable South African life, heating, transport and even shopping were new challenges. 'But it was a relief to be away from the threat,' she says.

She explains that, for Guy, it was initially a shock to move from living a highly politicised life to not having a central political role. Travelling by Tube to deliver the *Weekly Mail* was difficult for him. But once he started working for Afravision, things were easier. He was then in daily contact with South Africans about news footage that would often be aired on the BBC or ITV news.

For Jeanne, once she began working for IDAF, 'I felt a nice sense of commitment. We were getting a lot of news about what was happening. People were being detained. There was a sense that we were a whole lot better off than people back in South Africa. People in Grahamstown were undergoing long periods of detention. We both experienced a sense of guilt at being out of the country while other people were going through all these hardships. But we knew what we had been through with prison and the second detention. We were risking Guy losing out on seeing his children.'

There was a price to pay for refugee status, as grateful as they were to have it. Jeanne couldn't go back to South Africa without losing it, and Guy couldn't go back at all. Luckily, both sets of parents could and did visit them – Jeanne's once a year, Guy's rather less often.

* * *

With the release of Walter Sisulu[53] from Robben Island in October 1989 came their first thoughts of return. After twenty-five years in prison, Sisulu became deputy president of the newly unbanned ANC. Then, in February 1990, his fellow prisoner Nelson Mandela was released. Guy and Jeanne decided to stay in England a few months more, so they would have British residence and their British-born daughter Alexia would have citizenship.

The family went back to live in Cape Town, where Guy first worked at *New Era* and later *South*. Jeanne took a job with the Education Resources and Information Project at the University of the Western Cape, working with youth groups for three years before their return to Grahamstown, when Guy took the position at Rhodes. There he ran what became one of the most well-known journalism schools in Africa, promoting press freedom among students and in the wider society.

Seventeen years later came the job at UNESCO in Paris. And this is where I speak to him finally, two years on. Guy's contract has been renewed, he is just back from his Christmas holiday in Cape Town, and it is only a few weeks after Nelson Mandela's death.

Guy notes that for the previous five years, Mandela had been a background presence. 'It had, I suppose, a certain reassurance about it,' he says. The week before Mandela died, he and Jeanne attended the premiere of the movie *Long Walk to Freedom* at UNESCO. 'That was quite a moving thing in and of itself – we didn't know he was going to die. It brought a tear to the eye. It was an honest movie also in that it showed that this was a person who was all too human and in a different society would have carried on becoming a playboy and a rich businessman. The movie showed, I think, how that trajectory changed because he was forced to come to terms with discrimination against himself, but also, perhaps more importantly, to come to terms with what was happening to other people, and so he was forced to empathise with people less fortunate than him.

'It humanised him. The film shows how this took a toll on his first relationship, and interestingly enough, it shows he was violent as regards his first wife, and so it didn't romanticise him too much. That's all the more reason why the movie was strong, because it showed a person who was very much a product of his times, but he reacted in a way which ultimately was a blessing to the country and, of course, even more broadly.'

In the year leading up to Mandela's death, the only South African story abroad in France, says Guy, was the alleged murder of Reeva Steenkamp by the Paralympic athlete Oscar Pistorius. 'You have a classic South African violence story; then you have people coming to you and saying that Mandela had touched them. It was a remarkable thing.

'It reminded me of when we were students and Steve Biko was killed and [the minister of police] Jimmy Kruger said, "Biko's death leaves me cold".[54] So basically you have that position on the spectrum of responding to a black South African leader's death by saying it doesn't affect me at all, and then you have Mandela's death and so many people felt moved by this. I think what it did was to remind people symbolically about history, about someone who had dedicated his life to the cause of others and wasn't born like that but was shaped by society. And in a world where there is a lot of cynicism and materialism, issues of environmental degradation, poverty, and so on, to be reminded about values was not a bad thing at all.

'That's perhaps why Mandela's death was meaningful to me and to others, particularly with me now working in an international organisation, where international political dynamics are so strong and where there is a lot of rhetoric and with reality being somewhat different – to be reminded of somebody who walked the talk, I think that was a kind of a rare moment.'

I tell Guy that my daughter had texted me the news of Mandela's death as I sat alone in a London restaurant after work. I was so shocked I blurted it out to the Polish waitress who had come to my table. She dropped to her knees and threw her arms around me. 'I'm so sorry,' she said.

Guy had similar experiences. 'Many people came up to me as if I had had a personal loss in the family. It was moving to have people acknowledge me as a South African, particularly because the only South African in the news before that had been Oscar Pretorius, so it was like going from a rather distressing model of South Africans in the media to really feeling that as a South African one had a special status, because one had a more direct connection to Mandela.'

When you went to South Africa for your holiday, what was the reaction among people there?

'I think everyone was a little bit sobered by the experience. There was a reminder of where the country had come from – that for all the many, many, many problems, it is a damn sight better than it was. And that Mandela, who, of course, only stood for one term of office as president, had set the bar, and everyone else will be judged, politicians and citizens alike, on that standard.

'I think it's reinforced for many people the gap between the current leadership and Mandela's own position. But I think that it wasn't just a case of disillusionment. That legacy of Mandela – nobody was saying it was meaningless or it was a waste of time or it was worthless, but rather that it underlines the importance of trying to live up to it. Obviously, everyone was quite touched by this man and how he had gone through such a long period of history.

'But I think also there wasn't a complete romanticism, in that some of the people I spoke to thought that he hadn't dealt properly with HIV/AIDS during the first term of his presidency and that he could have made a difference at that early stage. And in terms of his economic policies, for example, he had been overstressing free markets when the society needed more Keynesian policies.

'I think it was an appreciation without a sentimentalisation, put it that way. It reinforced that one ought not to forget the trajectory that Mandela set out on, which was an ethical and a values-based trajectory, certainly a non-racial one, and also one that was concerned with the life and living conditions of the majority.

'These are issues that need greater attention, but there has been some progress. When we were travelling in the fairly remote Karoo on this recent trip, we saw these RDP houses[55] – you know, the ones the government has provided. They all had little solar-powered geysers on their roofs. Now certainly in terms of what one has come to associate with contemporary South Africa – that there is so much corruption, and so on and so forth – one doesn't know whether in the contracts for these solar heaters there was perhaps corruption there. It's not irrelevant, but the main point is there are solar panels on people's roofs so they now have hot water.

'It's the complexity of South Africa, just in the same way you have the Mandela funeral on one hand and then you have the saga of the sign-language guy.[56] All this is really South Africa, isn't it? It's a tale of incredible real sacrifice and real idealism on the one side, and then it's a tale of people who are odd to say the least and who find their way, amazingly enough, through the checks and balances and security into delicate and public-profile settings. The mix of the two – this tells us this is South Africa; it's not one or the other, it's both.

'At least Mandela's life did tower above everything else, even though the sign-language guy was in the news and understandably so. Nevertheless, Mandela still managed to be *the* main story.'

How do you think the South African media will fare under President Zuma if he tries to crack down on press freedom?

'There's a very strong civil society in South Africa, so the ANC would face a lot of opposition. Every time there is an outcry, they do back down. There is a different environment now; people do have rights. It would be hard to take them away – not like when I was a student and they could close down the main newspapers and people would be cut off from knowledge.'

What is your view of South Africa now and, particularly politically, what do you think the future holds?

'I continue to be optimistic because basically South Africans are so fractious; there are so many different interest groups. It's a strength of the society that the spectre of totalitarianism is so remote – that if one remembers back to the days of Vorster, who was this man of granite and was so forceful, and the government was just so monolithic and powerful, and now there is nobody who has that degree of potential power. Jacob Zuma is being attacked left, right and centre, even by his own people. There was a report by his own ministers about Nkandla [the issue of improvements to Zuma's private residence which were paid for by the taxpayers], which is not very complimentary.'[57]

'Of course, the trade unions are at loggerheads with him, and Julius Malema and his group[58] are also. So everyone is bickering with everyone else, and then, of course, you have the business community, you have churches, you have societies, you have individuals, you have Bishop Tutu, you have the different regional interests. This is actually quite fun; we obviously hanker after some sense of unity in South Africa – a rainbow shouldn't be so fractured that it would lead to civil war. Nevertheless, this cultural rainbow is really adjusting a very dynamic set of interests, and I think that's a good thing because the history of some post-colonial societies has been to go towards the great man and some sort of totalitarian control, and that definitely won't be the case in South Africa.

'Part of this rivalry is that it's also actually a foundation for creativity and innovation, as well as checks and balances. There are very few countries in the world, even quite long-established democracies, where a cartoonist like Zapiro[59] can exist and do his stuff, where a painter can paint a picture of the president with his penis exposed.[60]

'South Africa is a free country, and what is quite remarkable is that part of the freedom is that nobody can get full control of everything, even though at the same time one would like to see more control over crime and over corruption. There are mixed patterns in what kind of personalities are being appointed, what kind of institutions are being closed down or opened up, and what kind of laws are being passed. Sometimes it looks more depressing and sometimes it looks more optimistic, but I think on the whole it's held up. It's been nearly twenty years since democracy, and you still have the office of the public protector, which is still very independent although appointed by the government; you have the courts, which are still independent; and an independent journalism. So I'm quite positive about this.

'At the same time, where South Africa really needs to get its act together is in education. This is the biggest problem, I think, in terms of the society moving ahead, and it's the key to developing the kind of economy that can deal with poverty and unemployment and all the associated problems. Who would have thought that the education problem would have been so difficult to solve? Patently it has been, and it's not always through lack of having good people in charge of it. There are some departments that have become quite well respected. The South African Revenue Service is very efficient at chasing all kinds of bigwigs who have been doing tax dodges. But education leaves so much to be desired.'

Education, Guy says, needs to be 'not just put on a kind of manageable footing but geared towards the needs of the country, primarily fostering some kind of entrepreneurial capacity so that people can actually set up and run businesses, big and small. Otherwise, we are not going to solve this problem of unemployment, which is the biggest cause of social problems in the country. So I'm very optimistic politically, though I do think that we need a lot more work on the economy and particularly on education as a means towards improving the economy. And I don't think it's a case of just throwing money at education; it requires a lot more attention and management from the government side to what's happening in the schools.'

What has your role at UNESCO meant to you?

'Personally what it's meant is exposure to societies that have much worse conditions than South Africa. That's a very humbling thing. And at the same time, I do think that the exposure to South Africa has given me a lot of insight, which I can bring to bear in the work that I do vis-à-vis these other societies.

'The work I do is to promote freedom of expression and media development, so one of the things is awareness raising, and trying to encourage greater public and governmental appreciation of why freedom of expression is so important as a human value, a human right. And in practice, what that means is that freedom of expression is circumscribed violently, often in the killing of journalists. This can happen in war situations, but most killings of journalists do not take place in war situations.

'You have journalists being killed for exposing drug dealing in Mexico or illegal logging in south Asia, or some religious zealots taking them out in Pakistan. So one is dealing with the worst violation of freedom of expression, which is the ultimate censorship of those people. First of all, no one ought to be killed for exercising their freedom of expression. Second, it's not just an expression of those individuals' rights; it's because as journalists they are visible, they are in the public eye. So if a journalist is killed, the signal it sends out to those not even working in the media is that it is dangerous to speak out, and so you have the effect of intimidating the society more broadly.

'This is particularly pertinent in regard to women. If a woman journalist is killed, this definitely tells women at large that they live in a dangerous place: "Don't stand up and don't say what you really think. Don't blow the whistle on domestic violence, don't blow the whistle on corruption, don't stand up for secularism." To me this is a very important issue to work on, and we have found some societies where things have improved.

'And they have improved in different ways. One is public awareness raising, where communities start realising that this is not just a blow to individuals, but is something that is denying everyone their rights and is also reducing information of public interest, reducing the availability of public information to society. And you've got mobilisation, particularly by media people themselves, who are obviously directly interested in this, and then on the part of the government side. Sometimes governments pass laws that set up special units to investigate the killings of journalists and other times to set up protection, so if a journalist is receiving death threats, which often precedes the actual killing, there is state protection available.

'I'm speaking particularly here of Colombia in Latin America, where the number of killings of journalists has substantially declined, and so there are lessons one can take from there and propose to other countries and say maybe if you adapt this Colombian experience, you can begin to develop campaigns, advocacy, law reform and institutional reform, and you can deal with the issue of safety for journalists. So that's the kind of work I do. South Africa rarely sees journalists being killed these days, although intimidation and harassment are not uncommon. While this is not nearly as bad as it used to be, it is still of serious concern.

'At UNESCO, we are training security forces in Tunisia in how to respect journalists' work, and there is a code of conduct we have developed with them about this. The police training college in Tunisia now incorporates the idea that journalists should not be caught in the crossfire, and not be abused or intimidated or have their cameras confiscated, as well as why attacks on journalists should be investigated properly.

'To compare that to South Africa: in South Africa I was extremely sensitised to freedom of information and expression – I mean, I went to jail largely on a conviction for banned books, which they said indicated that I furthered the aims of a banned organisation. There were terrible cases of people who expressed themselves being banned and going to jail for five years, so I bring this value of having experienced an unfree society and just how important it is to have freedom of speech.

'These rights, they are not just given to you on a plate; you have got to have a culture that respects them. You've got to have institutions that can protect them. There is law reform that is needed to protect them; there is training needed for judicial people; and the media needs to be organised if it's going to effectively cherish and defend the role of journalists.

'So this is the stuff I bring from South Africa. When talking about the extensive transition in South Africa, this is quite useful as well, because first of all there is understanding the role of the media in a transitional situation, particularly when the media was formerly very divided in South Africa between the mainstream, which included the SABC[61] and so on, and the alternative press.

'Ultimately it is a story of developing a form of unity among all journalists, which is extremely important for actually advancing and defending freedom of expression. South Africa wouldn't have had such a good deal on freedom of expression, it wouldn't have necessarily have had some Constitutional Court rulings on issues like defamation, if it wasn't for an organised journalism community, and particularly through the editors. I used to be very involved in the South African National Editors Forum when I was head of the Rhodes University journalism school. It taught me that you've got to get the journalists united, despite all their differences and their historical divisions, because they have got to agree on one thing: that journalists have got to be free to do their work and that regulatory systems should protect them to do so. This is very useful for me when I am working with other countries where things are really tense and the media is divided.

'One new area I'm working on which I find quite challenging is the whole area of freedom of expression on the internet. Of course, this is a relatively new issue. We didn't have the internet under apartheid – if we had, maybe things would have been different, although no doubt the apartheid government would have tried to control the internet and use it for espionage.

'Today some governments will do the best they can to try to control freedom of expression on the internet, to a greater or lesser degree of success. There are lots of cases where bloggers have been jailed. There have been firewalls and censorship and blocking of sites. There have been cyber-attacks on media websites. There are also journalists' sources being exposed, even in democracies; subpoenaing of reporters' telephone records; and using all these electronic means to reduce freedom of expression.

'This is not just a question of national governments doing it now. You have the question of the whole internet being a global medium. And so it becomes a lot more complex. What is also interesting is that the internet is also very interpenetrated with other things, such as commerce, social life and personal life. In the old days, control of the media was control of one sector of society; it didn't mean you controlled the economy and it didn't mean you controlled people's personal correspondence. Today, the internet is increasingly all these things together.

'Because it's global, it is really complicated to figure out how to advise various actors on what kinds of checks and balances there should be. The argument on behalf of democratic country governments is that they need to be monitoring in case of terrorism. You can't dismiss this, because governments do have the duty to provide for the security of their citizens. At the same time, the potential for abuse is enormous. One only has to think what [US president Richard] Nixon would have done if his intelligence-gathering included all the information on the internet – not to mention what Edgar Hoover and the FBI would have done in smearing political opponents.[62] And that's in the US, which is such a long-established democracy, with all its traditions of rights and freedom.

'There is danger, therefore, in how states fulfil their obligations to protect people if it is at the expense of respecting and protecting their privacy and freedom of expression. And so this is something one has got to try to promote in terms of norms and values: an approach and understanding by all actors that as much as human rights should be respected offline, they should be respected online.

'In addition, any policies on the internet should not be made unilaterally by governments, because the internet is such a complex ecosystem. It's really got to be done in a participative way in discussion with stakeholders, which includes businesses and society, and intergovernmental agencies as well. You really need what they call in the jargon "multi-stakeholder governance" of the internet. If you have just one actor making decisions, i.e. governments or big companies, it's really not optimal for all the interests intersecting on the internet.'

Could you give me an example of where things have changed markedly for the better in one of the countries that you have worked with?

'Tunisia is a very good example of a country where there used to be a huge amount of censorship, cyber-censorship, cyber-attacks, espionage, and then jailings of people for their activities in cyberspace. And now Tunisia is one of the leaders in freedom of the internet globally. I was at a conference about a year ago where Google were explaining that they had blocked that controversial video *The Innocence of Muslims*.[63] They had blocked it in Pakistan and Egypt because the video was being used by extremists to mobilise for rioting.

'And the Tunisians said, "Who are you, Google, to make these decisions and to make this judgement call? We as Tunisians think our public are mature enough to deal with this kind of rubbish on the internet, and if there ever happens to be such a decision, we will take it, not you; you are not elected by Tunisian citizens. We are completely against this kind of censorship – our people are mature enough to cope with it."

'In fact, they don't censor at all in Tunisia. So that's a good example. This is the beauty of UNESCO, because it's an intergovernmental organisation: there are 195 governments represented there, and we can share good practices. It's complex, because they all have different interests, and so on. But at the same time, UNESCO has relations with other actors – business and civil society. So, for example, take the huge debate over the Edward Snowden revelations.[64] Civil society people came up with a set of guidelines for specifying under what conditions espionage would be legitimate: there must be independent oversight, and some transparency about the number of access requests; surveillance must be targeted, and must not be bulk surveillance, etc. They came up with all these principles and those are very worth considering, and at UNESCO we can bring these ideas to the attention of governments. We can advise that when you are designing your own regimes for how you will develop human rights–compliant espionage, this is what civil society is proposing.

'And so this is the kind of work we can do at UNESCO, which is getting that dialogue going between these different actors.'

It's a very powerful position to be in and an effective place to work. There's a neat kind of continuity with what you were doing before, with what happened to you in your earlier life, and then with your work at Rhodes and in Africa and now here. It must be quite good to look back on it all.

'I have been fortunate. I felt at the time Mandela died that I was quite privileged in a way. Although it was difficult, I was privileged to be part of a society that was undergoing change, that offered me an opportunity to be part of it and that it was successful. And I'm hoping that some of the work I can do at UNESCO can be successful – not for me as an individual, but as part of a successful movement.'

Do you feel now that it was all worth it?

'I would say yes, but you can interpret your question in two ways. The one is, was it worth it in terms of the result; and the second is, was it worth it just because it was the right thing to do?

'In terms of whether it was the right thing to do, I think yes, absolutely. I have such an abhorrence of racism that in a way I don't think I could have done anything different, particularly the way racism worked out in apartheid South Africa, in terms of such an extensive deprivation and humiliation; it was institutionalised so absolutely. Racism disgusts me so much; I feel very emotional about this, and this is the kind of thing that does drive one to action. It is just appalling. So was it the right thing to do to fight apartheid? Yes, absolutely.

'Was it worth it in terms of outcome? I don't think I personally achieved anything significant. It's hard to measure, especially because there were lots of individual contributions. Maybe what I did was significant in inspiring some other people to take action, for example, and that contributed ultimately towards sanctions being imposed on the South African government.

'Maybe the fact that I was a white activist helped in some ways to reinforce the perception among the ANC people that you should not judge people by the colour of their skin. We were not fighting as white people but fighting against racism. I'm speculating, but my role certainly wasn't a high-level contribution in that sense. Was it a measure of failure that I was caught?' He laughs. 'Maybe one should celebrate those who weren't caught. It's hard to say whether my action was worth it in terms of outcomes. But was it worth it in terms of whether it was right? For me, there is no debate.'

The whole outcome – in other words, the fact that we no longer have apartheid, that it's twenty years since a new democracy – was it worth it in that sense?

'In that sense, yes, there is no doubt about that. It's certainly not the perfect society that one probably naively thought could come about more quickly. It certainly could be better than it is, but if you take the longer-term view, it's a different world and a different country to what it was. And a much better one.'

This year is the twentieth anniversary of 1994. It's a big year, isn't it? There will be big reports out, there will be number-crunching.

Where is the society? Obviously in a better place. There will be a lot of interest worldwide and a lot of coverage, and it will be interesting to see what happens.

'Yes, I think people will take stock of twenty years of freedom. It's something to be cherished, that things have held together. What happened with liberation was that you took the lid off the pot. Had that lid stayed on, the situation would have become more and more pressured and headed towards a major explosion.

'South Africa is still boiling, it's still bubbling, but the steam can escape. The water remains in the pot, it's not going to burst out. That the fabric of society is still very fractious is part of why the pot keeps on bubbling; that's energy that has been created. It stops the mud from settling.' He laughs. 'If I continue the metaphor,' he adds, 'I certainly don't see any catastrophe looming in the wake of Mandela's death.

'The society is definitely strong enough, and now there is a democratic culture where people feel entitled to their rights and they will express them, even though not yet always in the most peaceful way. There is a sense that South Africans are entitled to democracy. And that's good – we've obviously got to deepen that and extend that sense of entitlement to others, particularly emigrants and refugees from other parts of Africa, but the basics are there and that's really good.'

PART THREE

Zubeida Jaffer

For the third part of my trip, I flew to Cape Town to stay with my old friend Barbara McCrea and her son Gabriel. We walked the path along the sea to the St James tidal pool and swam lengths in the cold, clear water as the glittering waves rushed over the wall and the sun shone on the sea beyond.

Just as we came to the pool, we saw an Asian bride and groom walking along the path. They were down to have their picture taken on the lawns by the sea, the bride in a beautiful pewter silk dress finely caught in at the waist and then dropping wide about her ankles and flowing behind her. 'You two look gorgeous,' Barbara said to them. 'May you be happy.'

The next evening we took a walk. As we came up the steps onto the road above ours, we saw two men: the guard hired to protect the residents' cars against break-ins, carrying a knife, and a man he was chasing away, down the stairs towards Barbara's flat.

We carried on rapidly, up past houses whose fences were topped with five strands of electric wire and defended by dogs. Then we came back down a series of stairs past a man sitting in the bushes with a bunch of plastic bags. Whether he was busy taking 'tik' (crystal meth, available for five rand a pop) or simply going through stuff he'd taken from rubbish bins, we didn't stop to enquire.

Back in the flat, I discovered on checking the news that the night before, while Barbara and I had enjoyed Cajun-style kingklip at the

Olympic Café in Kalk Bay, a British couple – Shrien and Anni Dewani – were hijacked in Gugulethu while in Cape Town on their honeymoon, and she was murdered. 'They were on their way back from a trip to the Winelands,' I wrote in my journal, 'and decided to drive through Gugulethu "to sample the nightlife" – this last phrase makes absolutely no sense to me, but I guess it's a mistake anyone in a strange land could make. He has South African relatives but I have to guess did not grow up here.'

I remember thinking, What on earth were they doing driving through Gugulethu at night? I realised at once that this was an extraordinary story and offered it to Fraser Nelson at *The Spectator*. Like many others, he thought it would blow over in days – not good for a weekly magazine – and so declined. They were all wrong: the British rat pack (which I had once briefly been part of) arrived within days and didn't leave for a long time, surrounding the magistrate's court at Wynberg where Shrien and the Dewanis' taxi driver appeared, mobbing the police cars, stalking the hotels where Shrien might be staying, retracing the doomed steps of the couple that night. The journalists were everywhere.

And now as I write, three years later, Shrien has, after a long legal battle, been extradited to face a murder charge in South Africa, where two men are already serving life sentences for the crime – two men who claim Shrien bribed them to shoot Anni. I could only imagine her terror in the moments between realising that something was wrong and the shot that killed her, whether or not it was her husband who ordered the killing.

Her murder captured the media's imagination and made headlines worldwide. There is still speculation about whether she was raped. Yet murder and rape are daily realities in Gugulethu and the other townships of South Africa. The statistics indicate that women who live in South Africa are more likely to be raped than to learn to read; one in nine women will be raped; there are up to 3 600 rapes each day.[65] Murder statistics are high too. Significantly, 81 per cent of these murders happen in black households – counter to the received wisdom that it is whites who are being targeted.

Yet the whites are nervous, and for a while I was one of them. I stayed with Barbara, going off to do my interviews, sharing her evening swims and sometimes cooking for her and her friends, sitting in the peaceful sunlit flat alone but for her pretty brown and white cat that was so like mine in Sussex, writing and writing, haunted by the stories I was hearing.

Then Barbara went to work in Joburg for a week, leaving me to cat-sit while Gabe went to his father. (The truth was that the cat didn't really need a sitter; I needed somewhere to stay.) The days were good: interviews, writing, swims on Muizenberg Beach and at St James. I learned to strip down to my costume and towel, lock everything else in the car and leave the keys with the surf shop, then head for the beach. That way there was no risk of my possessions being stolen while I swam, which had happened to a woman we met one day on the coastal path on her way back from the tidal pool. She was wearing a swimsuit and a borrowed towel: the rest had all vanished.

But the nights were different. I'd been advised that if I had been out for the evening, I should ring the armed security guard. He would meet me and ensure I got safely into the flat after I'd locked my car in the backyard. So far, so good. But then I would go to bed and, ever a poor sleeper, finally drop off, only to be woken in terror by loud thumping along the corridor followed by the cat landing hard on the bed – on me, in fact. I can laugh about it now, but one night I was so nervous I decamped to another friend's house.

I was in Cape Town to interview Zubeida. I had last seen her the year before, when I came out for the 2009 election and she had kindly organised my press accreditation. After my whirlwind day atop Helen Zille's election bus as the Democratic Alliance (DA) won the Western Cape from the ANC, she was my guide through the election centre for the excitement of the results that night.

Zubeida had given me a warm welcome, even though we had been no more than fellow students, and she hadn't seen me for thirty years. I was to learn that this warmth was utterly characteristic of her. On election night everyone knew her, from the new Anglican archbishop to the commissioner of police. There was a sense that everyone knew that here was a woman – a pretty, smiling, conservatively dressed fifty-year-old – who had put her life on the line for them more than once.

'Tell her the story,' said the commissioner. The story is that when he was a high school pupil and the son of a cleaner at the Rhodes University residences, Zubeida had coached him in maths; the moral of the story is that the new South Africa is about incredible mobility.

It is difficult to separate Zubeida Jaffer from her family – a large, strong, close-knit, Muslim family, which, when she was growing up, was at once traditional and politicised. Zubeida's mother, Raghmat, did not work outside the home; her hands, Zubeida recalls, were the hands of a woman who did the family's washing herself. Yet none of the family were allowed to attend any gathering where whites and blacks had to sit separately. Through them ran a deep antipathy to the apartheid system. Raghmat became the chair of the Wynberg branch of the United Women's Organisation, later to become the United Women's Congress (UWCO),[66] a grassroots organisation working in oppressed communities, earning her the disapproval of her in-laws and other family members.

There were already five siblings by the time Zubeida was born in 1958. She was the youngest and the most physically fragile, yet by the time she was just twenty-two, with a childhood of ill health and operations behind her, she became the first of them to suffer at the hands of two of apartheid's cruellest torturers – the notorious security policemen 'Spyker' van Wyk[67] and Frans Mostert.[68]

In Cape Town I am to meet Zubeida's two brothers, who are closest in age to her, and her redoubtable mother (her beloved father died in 2000). This is a family who were deeply traumatised by what happened to their baby sister, and who were galvanised into action by her arrest.

By the time Zubeida arrived at Rhodes University to enrol for the journalism degree, she had already completed a BA at the University of Cape Town. As a 'non-white' person she was allowed only to attend lectures and then had to leave campus; she was not allowed to take part in any social activities.

Rhodes should have been different, a better place. After all, she was there under the law that admitted black students to degrees that weren't available at black universities. Yet her attendance there pretty well pitched her straight into direct political action. Impressed with her academic record, Professor Tony Giffard had sought permission for her to complete her first year and second year concurrently. And for the first year, she and the four other black women students at Rhodes were accommodated in a whites-only residence. But at the end of that year they were thrown out.

'The government had told the university that blacks were not allowed in the residences,' Zubeida explains. 'Instead of the university standing up for us, they actually informed us that we had to vacate the residences. They were white liberals but they couldn't even protect their own students. So that was a very formative experience.'

Zubeida led the black students – the women and the twenty-five black men on campus – in a protest. It was her first experience of political action. 'In the end, the university decided to set up black residences for men and for women, and they approached me to be the subwarden of the women's residence. I refused because I felt it was so insulting – which meant I had to come back to Rhodes the following year with no place to stay.'

She met with the other black students. 'I told them to go into the residences because they had no option. But I just could not do it.' Instead, Zubeida found a derelict building next to a shop, located the owner, and persuaded her to fix the broken window and the door. She and friends painted it out, and she and her friend Ephne Williams lived there. Direct action: it was typical of Zubeida.

She has nothing but scorn for the university authorities. 'That was my central experience of Rhodes, that the university didn't stand up and protect me.'

This was only her first act of defiance in a decade of resistance, detention, torture and a life on the run. In later years she must have looked back on the quiet campus as a kind of oasis. 'I enjoyed the connection with the local community and the exposure to the Eastern Cape,' she says. She was also exposed to the Black Consciousness Movement, with its artists and poets.

'I was asked recently for a magazine interview, "Where were you happiest?" And I said, "At Rhodes." Why? Because it was the first time I was truly on my own and my first taste of adulthood. I've got a really soft spot for Rhodes and for Grahamstown too.'

Zubeida joined the *Cape Times*, a liberal Cape Town daily newspaper, after graduating in 1980, and within months had attracted the attention of the security police with an article about police shootings on the Cape Flats.[69] She was taken into detention, tortured and poisoned by Spyker van Wyk in July 1980. She was just twenty-two years old.

Years later, Zubeida told the Truth and Reconciliation Commission what Van Wyk did to her:

I hadn't slept for days. And they gave me some food ... And he said he was going away, but he was coming back again. And I started seeing ... I started seeing all my veins in my hands dilating. And my arms, my veins in my hands and my arms, and I ... I felt pains across my chest and suddenly I started feeling like ... all my insides were going to come out ... And I said to them, 'I am going to get sick ...' And the one guy ran to the toilet to take me, the other guy ran to the phone and he said, 'It's starting.' Now at that point I didn't think anything of it [that she was being poisoned], I was just seeing all my veins dilating, it looked like worms – it looked like worms coming out of my hands. It was all standing up. I thought my blood vessels were going to burst and I just felt these pains across my chest ... Then Captain Du Plessis came back and he said: 'Zubeida, you know, you are never going to make it, you're going to have a heart attack, you're going to die.'

They said, 'Zubeida, if you don't cooperate with us and tell us ... then we are going to detain your father.' And I thought they were just trying to trick me again. But then in the course of the morning they made a phone call and they called me to the phone ... and it was my father on the phone ... I was shattered at that point. I just felt that it's fine if they involve me, but why involve my family? And so after they put the phone down, I signed the statement ... And the effect of it all was that it completely humiliated me, it completely made me feel like I was worthless, that I had gone against everything that I stood for, that I believed in, and that I had been too weak to withstand the pressure.[70]

'After that detention, I became obsessed with changing the apartheid system,' Zubeida tells me. 'I couldn't really think of anything else. I felt that I'd been in the belly of the beast and I'd been confronted with the darker side of our country, and I was completely drawn into the mission of wanting to bring an end to that.'

And what was Zubeida charged with? Possessing three banned books – an offence for which she was acquitted. It's difficult to square this with the fact that she could have died.

The aftermath of this first detention was, she says, the worst. 'I didn't understand and I didn't get any psychological support. I was one of the first, if not the first, Muslim women from Cape Town to go through such an experience.' Her family was itself traumatised. 'It was a very lonely position to be in and most of the time I had to play the role of calming everybody down.'

Zubeida left the *Cape Times* in 1981. She played an important role in the resistance movement in the Western Cape and became a full-time activist, working with the Clothing Workers Union and later becoming a key organiser in the formation of the UDF, the major anti-apartheid movement of the 1980s. 'For the next ten years, we lived our lives on the edge,' she says, 'never knowing what was going to happen. And that has a certain impact on your psyche. Because you could die any minute.'

Five years on, there was a message from Winnie Mandela that Nelson Mandela would soon be released. A plan was hatched to produce thousands of flags in the ANC colours of green, black and yellow, so that even if celebratory gatherings were banned, people could hoist flags across the Western Cape. A scheme was hatched to make the flags in a factory, but on the last of five days of production there was a raid and everyone was arrested.

Two weeks after that, the pregnant Zubeida and her husband Johnny Issel were arrested in a side street, just two of 30 000 detainees over the next two years, and her nightmare began again.

This time, her interrogator was the equally notorious Lieutenant Frans Mostert. 'I have prepared a chemical for you to drink if you do not want to cooperate,' he told her. 'It will burn your baby from your body.' Zubeida didn't cooperate. She didn't want her daughter to know that in order to safeguard her life, her mother had given information about other activists. She told the Truth and Reconciliation Commission:

> Now this was a real threat to me because of the drug experience during my first detention. I knew that they could do it ... and so I sat there in my cell not knowing what to do. Eventually I decided not to give them any information because I felt that I didn't want my child to grow up with that burden on her ... if she is brought into this world thinking that her mother gave information so that she could live, that is a heavy burden for a child to carry. So I think that that unborn baby inside of me made it possible for me to be strong enough not to give in to their threats.[71]

Mostert did not get the information he wanted; Zubeida had called his bluff and she was released. But when he turned up at her house after her daughter Ruschka's birth, she went on the run with her baby, a way of life that was to last a decade.

In her memoir, *Our Generation*,[72] Zubeida described her horror as Mostert walked into her bedroom where she was resting with her baby:

I straighten the bedspread and lower my legs to the floor. The door creaks open … Then I see him. Pink, red face, light-brown hair, liquor-bloated body in a cream safari suit. This man who had tried to burn my baby from my body. He steps into the room in the direction of my child, his signature odour wafting towards me. I am screaming, shouting – but not moving.

'Get out! Get out! Dad, take him out of here. Don't let him look at Ruschka!' I turn my head from side to side looking for an object I can fling at him to protect myself. He steps back, grinning, as my father tries to persuade him to leave me alone. The hysteria surges up in me, taking over, snatching control of my body. I cannot think. The emotions are too strong. I follow him and my dad to the front door, shouting like a woman possessed until he leaves. Nothing can make me stay now. I have to find a place where I can be at peace with my baby. I have to.[73]

Zubeida went on the run after that. Her whole family, it seemed, were under siege. One of her older brothers, Adam, had been arrested, as well as her uncle Khalid Desai, and her youngest brother Mansoor was on the run. Adam had put up a poster in his butcher shop at Mansoor's request, calling for a work stayaway on 16 June 1986 to commemorate the tenth anniversary of the Soweto uprising; and her uncle, principal of one of the schools that were part of the student uprisings, had opened the building to students needing a place to meet. Within weeks of his arrest, Khalid was taken to hospital with a collapsed lung and a heart condition.

With the family gathered for the farewell ceremony for Zubeida's brother Sulaiman and sister-in-law Razia, who were going to Mecca, Zubeida was suddenly overcome by tears:

Yes, this has been going on for six years now. After my detention and torture as a reporter at the *Cape Times*, the security police became a constant feature in my life. They were there when I got off the train in the mornings on my way to work. They were there to slap a further subpoena on me as I stepped down from the dock after being acquitted for the possession of three banned books. They withdrew my passport the day after I reported that students at the University of the Western Cape had burnt an apartheid flag and raised an ANC flag. It was endless.

... I cry for my child, my husband, my family and my comrades. Zerene cries for her Adam ... Aunty Jane is crying for her Khalid, whom she fears may be dying ... Through the house and outside on the stoep, men and woman, young and old, shoulders touching, cry for their own personal anguish and for ours.[74]

Yet for Zubeida, this was only the beginning of life on the run. Mostert seemed to haunt her, but she never gave up. She recalls grabbing him by the lapels and screaming at him as he raided her mother's house while Johnny was visiting Ruschka; what Mostert didn't know is that her brother Mansoor was also there. She screamed and held onto Mostert; he ran into the house with a cocked gun; her mother set off the burglar alarm; pandemonium ensued as more policemen arrived, unsure whether they were attending a burglary or an arrest. Johnny and Mansoor escaped. Neighbours and schoolchildren gathered; Zubeida and her baby were flung into a police van – again.[75]

A few years ago, Zubeida was asked by the National Prosecution Authority whether she wanted to prosecute Mostert (Spyker van Wyk had died). Mostert had declined to give evidence to the Truth and Reconciliation Commission, which would have guaranteed him immunity. But Zubeida says she had become obsessed with the notion of how to break the cycle of revenge, 'of how to heal myself in order not to pass the burden of this on to my daughter'. She decided not to take up the offer.

'I said they had already taken ten years of my life. And I didn't want to give more of my life to them. I wanted to be free of them. In my mind they were just small men in the overall scheme of things, little cogs in the wheel. And what was important was to discard the apartheid system. The more I see the situation improving here, if I see

African people confident and I see my daughter not being a second-class citizen, then that for me is my vengeance.'

It's impossible to fault her logic, but equally impossible to hear this without a faint sense of regret. Mostert went into the private security business; like many of apartheid's henchmen, he has essentially got off scot-free. He wanted to meet Zubeida but she refused, although her former husband Johnny (who died in 2011) did meet him.

Zubeida, however, has reached a happier place. She has continued her work as a journalist and writer, and has received a clutch of international awards. *Our Generation* received high praise from Nadine Gordimer, who described it as 'vivid, essential testimony ... invaluable to us, which can come only from those remarkable people to whom South Africa owes its freedom'. Zubeida is still active in community politics. She has built a house in the garden of the childhood home that was so often raided by the police. When I first see her in 2009, her daughter Ruschka is studying law at the University of Cape Town and has just voted for the first time. Zubeida is about to go off to a writers' retreat in Switzerland. In later years she is to be writer in residence at the University of the Free State, while still active as a journalist and blogger.

But, perhaps unlike Mostert, she is still paying the price of those torture sessions. On my first visit I photograph her for the *Observer* article I'm writing. It's a photograph I enlarge, and while looking at it with my son, he sees what I had not: she is smiling, but the nails of one hand are pulling painfully (and possibly unconsciously) on the back of the other hand. The eyes and the mouth are saying, 'I'm fine', but the hands are telling a different story.

I learn later that she still suffers from post-traumatic stress disorder. It has hit her hard every thirteen years since the first arrest – that's three times so far. It seems that of the three Rhodes students (and Guy and Marion both individually assert this) Zubeida has suffered the most; yet she has remained resolutely determined to continue with meaningful work – her journalism, her writing, her activism and, when I saw her in 2010, her job as assistant to the minister of economic development Ebrahim Patel, which she had taken on for two years.

Guy has strong memories of Zubeida: he was one of those whom she had been urged to betray. 'Her friendliness was immediately apparent, and without clashing with her dedication to justice,' he says. 'She was arrested, tortured and called to give evidence against me for the "distribution of banned literature". There was no way she could ever have agreed to that, and eventually they let her go – although not without trying to charge her for the same offence.' The courts had called several people as witnesses against Guy; conscious of the dilemma this would present them with – refusal would mean imprisonment – he deliberately pleaded guilty. Both Guy and Zubeida, then, made sure to protect their fellow freedom fighters.

Guy has enormous respect for Zubeida. 'Unlike several other students picked up in connection with me,' he says, 'the police had not succeeded in breaking Zubeida. Some fifteen years later, she was in a different state – suffering enormous trauma after years of activism on the run, and the stress that her then partner might be killed. It took another ten years before she recovered sufficiently for her old personality to reassert itself.'

* * *

Behind every strong woman, there is inevitably another one – her mother. And Zubeida was blessed in being born to Raghmat Jaffer.

I drive to Wynberg to see Raghmat. She lives with her elder daughter, Dr Julie Jaffer. It's a quiet suburban street; the houses are long and low, set in neat lawns. I turn off the engine and listen to the silence. It's all so safe and quiet here. Yet, this family has been through so much.

Inside, the house is cool, shaded and tranquil. Raghmat Jaffer is a slim and regal presence, her hair pulled back into her trademark chignon. She does not look her age – she will be eighty-five the next day.

My first sighting of her had been in the framed photo on Zubeida's kitchen counter, which shows her carrying the Olympic torch in 2004 and grinning happily under its weight, wearing the regulation Olympic tracksuit. And my first meeting with her was at the Houses of Parliament, when she had come to an event on food security that Zubeida was hosting; immaculately dressed, she had looked as proud as any mother would in the circumstances. There was no inkling of what she and her daughter had been through in the years of apartheid.

She leads me through to her study, where our interview is conducted. She sits behind a large desk, upon which she has laid out carefully the items she wants to show me. They are the evidence every proud parent might gather for a visitor: photograph albums, newspaper cuttings. Yet the collection includes evidence of horror: the news photographs of her just-released daughter, looking far younger than her twenty-two years, with the marks of fear still clear on her face; Raghmat's own diaries that she kept throughout those years; and finally, a collection of letters, written carefully in tiny script on fragile lengths of toilet paper. They are carefully preserved under plastic, and have been painstakingly transcribed by Zubeida's father Hassan, who died in 2000.

In post-apartheid South Africa, it is difficult to comprehend the lengths to which Raghmat had to go in order to protect her daughter. The shock of Zubeida's first arrest was followed by her parents' desperate attempts to find out where she had been taken, to continue to have contact with her, and to maintain contact with her persecutor, Sergeant Spyker van Wyk. The Jaffers were a religious, respectable, hard-working family, whose children had grown up chafing under the bonds of apartheid and had been encouraged to stand up against the oppressive regime, and whose mother was founder and chair of the the Wynberg branch of the cross-racial women's group UWCO. Yet Raghmat was a devout Muslim who would not normally have spoken at length to any man outside her family, and who never, ever, left the house without her headscarf.

By the time she had her daughter back safely with her, a daughter so traumatised by her ordeal that she could not sleep alone, a daughter who would be forced to go on the run with her newborn baby girl, Raghmat herself had been transformed by her own private hell: the hell of not knowing whether Zubeida was dead or alive. And to this trauma was added the knowledge that Zubeida, so strong in mind, had never been strong in body.

'Zubeida was ill as a child,' Raghmat explains. 'She had an infection in her hip, so we had to nurse her back to health. She was in traction for three months. She couldn't go to school, but every day one of the children came to bring her lessons from her teachers, and at the end of the year, she passed. It was a great achievement.'

Zubeida's physical fragility is still a factor in her life today. But her determination would help her in detention, especially when facing the intractable Spyker van Wyk. 'Even now she's inclined to pick up illness,' says Raghmat. 'Physically sometimes she's not great, but her inner strength has gotten her through a great deal.'

And despite the family's determined stance against the system, the arrest itself was still a great shock. 'For us, we were a middle-class family; and for me, I'd never even been to a police station. I had led such a sheltered life. For something like this to happen, fighting with the security police, it was terrible. It had a profound effect on all of us. But I'm glad it didn't knock me over. We took it running straight despite all that.'

Any family is protective of its daughters. And Zubeida was only twenty-two and physically fragile. 'It was awful,' Raghmat admits with understatement. And most awful was the monster Sergeant Van Wyk.

But a mother, in defence of her children, fears nothing. 'I had to go to face him,' Raghmat tells me. 'I had a certain modus operandi. I used to get up in the morning, pray and dress myself beautifully – make-up and all that. Then I drove the car slowly to Caledon Square [police station]. I said to myself afterwards, "What are you doing?" But I needed to do that because those people were murderers.

'They wouldn't say where she was. When I faced Van Wyk, I had to play humble and tell him I didn't want to interfere in his investigation, that I just wanted to see my daughter to know that she was all right.

'He said I couldn't see her but that I could send her food. He actually softened, this monster. It was almost as if God was with me. So that's what I did. I used to go through a game, all dressed up and smart to go to the police station to deliver the food. But she wasn't there.' She looks bleak. 'That's just what I had to do.'

Raghmat clearly doesn't want to make the story about her instead of Zubeida. 'I had various adventures,' she says, 'but I think we'll just leave it on the back burner because it's distressing. But I was willing to do that for her. She was my child.

'Not knowing where she was: that was horrific. Really terrible. With ordinary criminals, there are visiting hours. You can visit them. For political prisoners, there's no such thing. They were kept totally incommunicado. That was the scary thing. Are they still alive? Are they still there? You don't know.

'Advocate Dullah Omar, who became minister of justice [in the post-apartheid government], was our legal adviser. He was a friend of the family, so he took everything personally. He eventually said to me that I had managed to do something he couldn't have done, because they agreed that we could send her some food!'

It's clear that a grudging respect began to build in the torturer for the mother who simply wouldn't give up. But then Zubeida was moved to Port Elizabeth, 450 miles away.

'We had gone in to see her. Julie was quite far pregnant with her second son. We went to hang around as they wouldn't let us in. I can still remember the gates onto Caledon Square where the police cars come in and out. Julie was in her car, on the opposite side. We were all lurking; we didn't know what we were doing. Then the gates opened and a police car came out.

'There were two cops in the front and a policewoman sitting in the back with Zubeida. The car came down and passed me. The child was so frightened. She said after that she cried and cried. The policewoman asked her what she was crying about, and she said she had seen her mother. And the woman said to her that she should have thought about before doing the things she had. She hadn't really done anything!

'And the next minute – this was really dramatic – Julie's little green Mazda raced around and chased after the police car down the street to the robots. The robots changed and the police car sped through, leaving her behind. I asked Julie what she was trying to do and she said she was trying to get to her sister.

'We were totally devastated that day to see her in the clutches of these monsters. We were right to be concerned, because they did torture her when she was in P.E.'

Zubeida has told me what they did to her in Port Elizabeth. She did not give in, but as her mother explains, 'Eventually she was charged with having banned books. My husband Hassan was called into the police station and he was questioned, and they put Zubeida on the phone. She was scared. She said, "Please give them the books".'

The books were in a case that the family had hidden in their service station in Grassy Park. But the police took Zubeida's father to her house, and then on to Grassy Park to get the books. 'They wanted to lock her up for a long time,' Raghmat says. 'So I got on the phone and called my son and daughter and told them to find the case and take it away. So they did. Then I had to phone them again, with the cops on the way, to tell them to bring the case back. They did, but they managed to break the lock and they took out some of the things. I'm sure Zubeida can tell you the names of the books.

'That was so terrible, to put one through all of that – so much pain and suffering. I couldn't eat or sleep. I was just thinking about where my child was. I would wake up in the night and cry. But the case story was the one we laugh about because it was so ridiculous.'

And this is what surprises me most during these interviews. I hear stories of terror and torture, I hear the voices of frightened parents. But there is always laughter too, laughter that shines against the darkness.

Your son Mansoor told me you were always political in that you were anti-apartheid, but that Zubeida's detention galvanised you.

'It changed me a lot. I was always a very private person and busied myself with my family. And then all of a sudden, I found myself in the middle of the road, chasing after the police like a mad person when they grabbed Zubeida and the baby for the second time. It changed my personality a great deal. Events like this have a great impact on one's own psyche.'

The family would phone ahead and arrange to take food down to the police station for Zubeida. But one day they were in the waiting room of the police station and heard a familiar voice. 'Zubeida seemed to have heard my husband's voice. She wanted us to know she was there, so she said a prayer in Arabic and she sang it out loud: the morning praise to the Prophet. And we knew it could only be her. Van Wyk was furious and ordered us all out.

'That man became so angry. He was the bane of our life. Now we sit here and laugh about it, but it wasn't a laughing matter at the time. He spoke in Afrikaans, but I insisted on speaking in English, and he couldn't always follow me. It was all part of the battle.'

So you were very private and then you become a tigress.

'Yes, especially because Zubeida had been so ill as a little girl, but we'd gotten her through it. She was in danger and her life could be taken.

'And we had to put up with a lot of flak from some relatives and some of the neighbours around. They used to say, "Such good parents, but look what the children are doing." We just used to say that they weren't committing crimes – they were fighting injustice.

'I came in for a lot of criticism. I was involved in the women's movement and went on a lot of marches. My in-laws thought it was not nice for Aunty to be walking in the street. I thought, Well, you get off your butt and walk in the street – and then Aunty can stay at home. They weren't politically aware. We had to contend with that sort of thing. That changed a bit when Mandela came.

'But the people of Wynberg were amazing. They gave us a lot of support. They also organised a petition, and we put people at the mosques calling for Zubeida's release. We tried to do what we could, but we were very limited in what we could do.'

During her second arrest, Zubeida found a pen in a case of clothing her mother had sent to her. 'She thanked me,' Raghmat tells me, 'but I didn't purposefully put it there. It must have fallen in. Then she started writing letters on toilet paper, dating them all.

'They used to take her to the district surgeon because she was pregnant. My husband, daughter and I went into town because we had some hint she was going to be taken to the surgeon, and then she came around the corner with these cops in attendance and spotted her dad. Before they could do anything, she ran over and put these things in his pocket. They pulled her away. She planned to share the letters with someone, anyone, and give them a note to get the letters to us. But there was her dad. It was a miracle.'

The family succeeded in doing it a second time. Raghmat went to the district surgeon with Adam's wife Zerene, hoping to see Zubeida. 'Zerene was also pregnant and quite nervous. But the two of us went in. I had been to Mecca and so throughout my adult life I had always worn a scarf. On that day I was there without my scarf, but with a hat on. The cops knew me, so I had to be in disguise.

'But they didn't know Adam's wife, so she went up in the lift to see the surgeon. There was a cop upstairs who wanted to know why she was there. She told him she was there to see a doctor, but was told that he had gone somewhere. Next minute she's back in the lift, and she sees Zubeida with the cops and they all go down together. They don't talk, but Zubeida puts a wad of letters in her hand.

'So that was it. Zerene came back with the letters, shaking. I really praised her for doing that. She was amazing that day. I couldn't have done that. She wasn't very political, but she followed the family. The letters that came through gave us some kind of link, so they were consoling in some way.'

And there they are thirty years on: faded but still legible – just – under the protective covering of plastic sheets. Letters that Zubeida planned to give someone – anyone – or just drop in the street with a note pleading with whoever found them to post or deliver them to her parents. A miracle? Yes.

We look at the letters together. I hold one in my hand, afraid it will disintegrate. I lay them out and photograph them, planning to look at them more closely later. It's extraordinary to think of that young woman alone in her cell, carefully writing in an almost microscopic hand, hiding the letters when she heard anyone approaching, and knowing there was nothing but the slightest chance of her parents ever receiving them. And not knowing whether she would make it out of prison alive.

And yet they did. And she did.

'You see,' says Raghmat, holding my gaze, 'one can overcome all these things. There must have been some kind of divine intervention, because all of these things happened – and we didn't organise them.'

'Do you think your faith helped?' I ask.

'Yes,' she says simply.

Then I ask if she thinks Zubeida's experience made her more political.

'It did,' she says without hesitating. 'One of the lessons we are taught religiously is that one of the disciples asked the Prophet, "After God, who comes first?" and the Prophet replies, "The mother". Then the disciple asks again, the second and the third time, and each time the Prophet replies, "The mother". Only when he asks the fourth time does the Prophet reply, "The father". So you see, Muslim women have status. The men can't make decisions without us.

'I got very involved with the UWCO, which brought all the mothers together. We worked very hard to protect women and stand together when children were detained. A lot of people broke down when their children were lugged off to prison. We had to be there for each other.

'Apartheid put us all in boxes, but in the UWCO all mothers came together – white and black. We got to know each other. It changed our minds. White people had been our enemies, but they became our friends and comrades. Our mindset had to change. There were major lessons to be learned, so some good things came out of that time too.'

The Jaffer family – two girls and four boys – had a more politicised upbringing than many Muslim families in Cape Town. 'Zubeida told me you didn't go anywhere that was segregated,' I say to Raghmat.

'Yes, the children lost out on quite a lot because we wouldn't go to those places,' she admits. 'They had that grounding and they grew up with it. They missed out on parties. They were in the townships, putting their lives at risk, being chased by the police, being locked up. We were proud of them, but I think we could have done without it all in our lives.'

Adam and Mansoor – Zubeida's brothers – were detained as well. 'It was hard on Adam's wife because she's a gentle person, but she had to run the butcher's with me,' says Raghmat. 'Adam said it was good he got released when he did; otherwise there would have been no business left, because we didn't know what we were doing!' She laughs.

'It was really ridiculous why they locked Adam up. He had two posters in the butcher shop commemorating the first day of the Soweto uprising, 16 June 1976, the day Hector Pietersen was shot. And they put him away for six weeks.

'Mansoor was detained twice. By the time they had both been detained, things were starting to lighten up a bit and starting to change, which is why it was such a shock when Zubeida was detained again. We were totally traumatised. We thought we'd been through it all. When they detained Adam, I went to the police station and Mostert was terrible. He had it in for us. He did it on purpose.

'The police called me in to ask me why we didn't know where Zubeida had been when she was on the run. She was on the run for quite a long time.

'She was with Ruschka at my son's home when Mostert arrived in 1986. Then she had to go off with the baby. It was so hard for her and so hard for me. I couldn't even be there when she was giving birth. I can't forget that. She was a new mother on the run. She had good friends who helped, but I couldn't know where she was.'

I hesitate to ask this, but I ask it anyway. *When you look back at it now, was it all worth it?*

'I feel that a lot of the youth don't understand what was going on then. My grandchildren's friends don't understand. I don't think we should be angry with them for that. The most important thing is that they're all having much better opportunities now. That's so gratifying. It makes everything all worthwhile. They can go to university. Everything's opened up. They can walk around with people of other colours and classes. It's rewarding.

'And mothers contributed a little bit to democracy and opportunities for all. I've been to my granddaughter's graduation and I sat there thinking how amazing it is. They let everybody in. How wonderful! It's about us. About the people. I feel it has been worth it.'

I have another question to ask: *Do you feel as a whole family that you've contributed to the great change that has come?*

'The thing is, everything just evolved,' Raghmat replies. 'I don't want to take credit. We made a contribution and that's great, but it was an evolution too.'

Finally, I ask Raghmat if, when she looks at South Africa today, whether she has any concerns. 'Certainly,' she says, 'but there are some things that get said in the newspapers about things being better then, but that's not true. Things are better now.'

* * *

Mansoor is Zubeida's closest brother in age – just a year younger. I meet him at his house in Wynberg and we walk to a café nearby. Like all the family, he is engaging, warm, funny, self-deprecating. We settle into comfy armchairs in the quiet of a back room, with a pot of rooibos between us, and talk.

Do you feel that what happened to Zubeida changed how you felt, or were you there already?

'I think it was a major trigger in our political consciousness. It was important, because in a sense it brought the issue of apartheid home. It really personalised it. It wasn't something that was happening to other people out there, but to someone who was very dear and close to us.

'In that sense, it was a major trigger in terms of our own political consciousness and our decision to become very active in the anti-apartheid struggle. But, of course, our development politically started way before that, as a result firstly of the experiences we had as people living in South Africa, and secondly as a result of some of the discussions that used to take place in our home – normally in very hushed tones.

'The sixties and seventies specifically were periods of great intensity in a way, because there was this psychosis of fear – I think probably because of the huge repression. That is my recollection when I think back to being a young person. Politics was something to be discussed quietly. There was always fear of repercussion and that the security police could be watching or listening and that you could suffer hugely as a result of holding political views.

'I think that was a result of the huge repression that took place in the sixties, with the banning of the ANC, the PAC, the detentions, and so on. One particular event that sticks in my mind is the death of Imam Abdullah Haron [the anti-apartheid activist and Muslim community leader murdered by the security police] in 1969. I attended the funeral with my late dad, and I can remember looking down on this huge mass of people and knowing that something was seriously wrong with the country.'

Zubeida recalled this occasion in her memoir:

In the distance, I saw thousands upon thousands of men winding their way behind a funeral bier bearing the Imam's body. My father was somewhere in that crowd. They had walked about twenty kilometres from City Park stadium in Athlone, where the funeral was held, to the cemetery in Salt River. By choosing to walk that distance, they had found the only legitimate way they could to voice their outrage.

Nobody knew the details of his death. All we knew was that he had died after being in police detention for 133 days and that his body was covered in multiple bruises, twenty-eight in all. The authorities said that he had accidentally fallen down a flight of stairs.[76]

The imam had been tortured by Spyker van Wyk, who, scarcely a decade later, was to interrogate and poison Zubeida. And less than a decade after the sight of the funeral cortege winding through Cape Town came the Soweto uprising in 1976.

'It had a profound effect on me,' says Mansoor. 'I was about seventeen, in Standard 9. That had a huge impact – the Soweto uprising through to the revolt of the rest of the country. Also in the Western Cape, I recall visions of thousands of people lining up in the streets, many people sporting Afros and Black Consciousness symbols. I remember driving with Adam, going out to see what was happening. All was not well.

'Of course, in 1980, the detention of Zubeida was the straw that broke the camel's back.'

That must have been a horrific time for your family because when people disappeared in detention then, no one ever knew what was going on. Your brother told me how he drove from police station to station. Your parents must have been distraught.

'Absolutely. I think that when something happens to your child, it touches you in more ways as a parent, and, of course, we can only appreciate that now as parents ourselves. It really took its toll on my parents. They were very distraught at the time and so were all of us.'

Mansoor was detained twice. The first time, in 1985, he was held in solitary confinement for twenty-eight days under Section 29 of the Internal Security Act.

'Previously, when Zubeida was detained, it was called the Terrorism Act. It was changed as a bit of PR – a bit of Goebbels-speak. Nonetheless, it allowed for indefinite detention – detention without trial and with solitary confinement.

'By that time I was a full-time political activist. I was working for the *Grassroots* community newspaper and was involved with the UDF, the youth organisations, underground work, and so forth.'

The UDF was officially a legal organisation, formed to combat apartheid. Yet thirty-five people in all were detained, says Mansoor, in the maximum security section of Pollsmoor Prison, including Dullah Omar, who later became minister of transport, and Graeme Bloch, Christmas Tinto and Shirley Gunn, all luminaries of the struggle.

So you were kept in solitary confinement for twenty-eight days. What about interrogation? Were they pretty hard on you?

'There was no physical torture, but psychological torture, yes. The lights were on twenty-four hours a day. At one point they put a gun against my head and pulled the trigger. They used to do mock executions. It was quite common.'

Did you manage to have any contact with any other prisoners?

'In prison, because you have a lot of time, you become very creative. I remembered this movie I had seen called *Papillon* – about a prisoner played by Steve McQueen escaping from Devil's Island. I'd seen the movie and read the book. The one thing that struck me was that he'd had this conversation through the toilet, through the pipes, with another prisoner in another section. So I decided to give that a try one day. I managed to get a message to this guy, Llewellyn McMaster [now Dean of Stellenbosch University]. I'd never met him, but I'd read a lot about him as he was always in the news. So I knew him quite well from his public persona.

'Then I had encountered this other prisoner, a guy that used to clean the corridors. He came past my cell one day and I asked him to take a note to Llewellyn, asking him to clear out his toilet at 5 o'clock that night, because that was when the wardens changeover – one goes off and another comes in – and you don't see them for close to an hour. I thought that would be the best time to speak to Llewellyn. After five, we had a conversation and became acquainted with each other through the toilet.'

It took Mansoor an hour to clear out all the water in his toilet. 'I only had an aluminium cup and a cloth. So I used to wring out the water, a little bit at a time. Presumably, he did the same thing. Once the water was almost all gone, you could hear the echo from the pipe and then we could make contact. It was better than any mobile phone I've ever encountered. The only thing I was fearful of is that the guards would see me with my head in the toilet and drag me off to an institution.'

So you never got caught?

'No, we just did it the once.'

It was quite a lot of trouble to go to.

'I'm not sure why we went to all the effort. It must have been towards the end of our stay or something. I'm not sure.'

Did you meet him again after you were released?

'Yes, we've got a good connection. We used to see each other. The activist community was like a family. We used to meet each other all the time.'

So many people were killed during the apartheid era. A look at the list of victims on the Truth and Reconciliation Commission website gives a flavour only of those whose stories were told. Yet there are always those whose stories haunt us.

For Mansoor, it was a man called Ebrahim Carelse. He was an ordinary man, no one famous, just another victim. 'When I was detained at Caledon Square, I saw a front-page story in the *Cape Times* of a man who'd been shot in Salt River. I'll never forget his name: Ebrahim Carelse. It was 6 September 1985, and I remember the date because that was the day I was detained. I think he died a few days afterward.'

Why was he shot?

'He was shot in the uprisings that took place when there was police action in Salt River. He was shot while trying to run into his home – a father of two children.

'In prison, you're not allowed access to newspapers, so for close to thirty days I didn't know what was happening outside. There was a complete blackout. But I managed to smuggle in one or two newspapers when I was inside. I had to pay one of the convicts R5 for a copy of the *Cape Times*.

'One article I saw said that my mother and my wife Kay had marched to Caledon Square for my release and the release of the other political prisoners. It quoted my wife shouting at the cops. That was quite something to see, being there in solitary confinement.

'But when I came out, I heard Ebrahim Carelse had died about three or four days afterwards, I think on 10 September. At his funeral, this policeman, Constable Farmer, was parking alongside the road and he was killed by the crowd. He was coloured. There were two policemen; one pushed off. Then this guy Farmer took out his gun and he shot someone in the stomach. And then people turned on him and they killed him right there. I wasn't there but it sounded awful and tragic.'

This story is just one of the many needless tragedies that littered the apartheid years. Coloured and Asian policemen were often seen as traitors to the cause. It's basically the same story that his older brother Adam is to tell me a few days later: the difference is that Adam was there when it happened.

Shortly after his release, Mansoor was detained again on 25 October 1985, under Section 50 of the Internal Security Act that allowed for detention for fourteen days. 'The reason why they used that is because a State of Emergency was going to be declared the following day and they just wanted to catch us in case we ran off and went into hiding. Before we could do that, they arrested us. And then the next day they "released" us. They didn't physically release us, but they told us that we were released under Section 50 but were being held under the State of Emergency. This time, I was with nineteen other people.'

The first time they detained you, what were they interrogating you about?

'About my involvement in the UDF. I generally got the sense that by that time, they were chasing after so many people that, unlike in 1980, at the time of Guy and Zubeida, or in the 1960s, when so few people were involved, I think we were in a position of relatively more security in some sense.

'They didn't really know much about everyone who was there. So they seemed to be fishing a lot. Some of the things they were asking me were really rather laughable. But then they also asked about some of my military activities and some of the people I'd been connected with, and about arms and ammunition.

'But they were speaking about generalities rather than specific stuff that they knew, and I could sense that from the start. They didn't really push anything. With Zubeida and Guy, they really wanted specifics out of them. With us, it was a little bit different.'

Did you get any sense at that time that the regime was coming to an end in any way?

'I know that we all thought it was going to go on forever.'

Did you feel any sense of desperation from them? Or loss of direction? You say that they didn't know what they were looking for necessarily.

'I think we generally felt emboldened by what was happening around the country, in the sense that by the eighties so many hundreds of thousands of people were participating in the resistance. I think that because of the time we lived in, we always had a sense of optimism. Our commitment to the struggle was such that we believed there was going to be change.

'However, we also saw that the state was very, very strong, especially militarily. Off and on we'd have doubts about the length of time it was going to take to reach our goals. But I don't think that most of us ever thought that by 1990 negotiations would have begun. In fact, it took most of us by surprise when it did happen. I'm sure it was the same for you over in the UK. You didn't expect it to happen so quickly.'

Mansoor's second detention was relatively short, about two weeks. 'And at that point,' he says, 'we could sense they knew even less. Craig Williamson was sent into our prison. We saw him. But the interrogation was very erratic and clearly not based on good intelligence. Three of us were released first from that cell, and that in itself showed that they didn't really know what they were doing. Because within the cell itself, we were among the most senior political activists and there were guys that had just been picked up off the road – perhaps students who had just engaged in militant action.

'We were let go. One guy who was released with me had been at Robben Island for six years before that. His name was Mzonke Jack. His nickname was Pro because he was such a good soccer player. He was really the veteran in our cell and he was released first, with myself and Ryland Fisher, who later became the editor of the *Cape Times*. We were released together and they dropped us at Bellville Station, which is about 25 kilometres from our homes. They just dropped us there. But Pro Jack was assassinated a few years later. Ryland's still around. He's running his own business now.'

What was happening and what you were involved in that they would have loved to have known about?

'We were members of the UDF, legally. We were also involved with the ANC underground, promoting its programmes and symbols. We were building mass democratic structures, as they were called – youth organisations. Zubeida was involved with the trade unions. Adam was involved in the business organisations – such as the butchers' association.'

Mansoor confirmed what Guy and Devan had told me: 'It was an important component of resistance in the eighties, the fact that business people also came on board and they would support consumer actions. There was a meat boycott in 1980. There was a Wilson Rowntree's boycott, there was a bus boycott. The small traders actually supported these actions and they were part of the UDF.

'And then we were involved with the *Grassroots* newspaper. *Grassroots* was started in the late 1970s by progressive journalists in Cape Town. I joined it in 1983. Initially I was what was called the news-gathering coordinator. Of course we didn't use titles like editor or deputy editor then. I was basically the news editor. In 1984 I went to Oudtshoorn to live for six months and I started a newspaper there called *Saamstaan* [Unite].'[77]

The move to Oudtshoorn shows Mansoor's dedication to the cause: the town was in the Afrikaner heartland, many miles inland. 'It's one of the hottest parts of the country, but one of the coldest in the winter. It's also probably one of the most conservative places in South Africa – after Potchefstroom. There was an army base there, very militarily repressive.

'Essentially, I was involved with *Grassroots* for five years, including the stint in Oudtshoorn. There are a lot of stories linked to this period of repression: the newspapers being closed down, the offices being burnt down, journalists being shot, journalists being detained.

'I was also with the youth organisation called the Cape Youth Congress when I was young and had lots of hair, like Guy Berger. The Congress was an umbrella body of different youth formations, geographically based. I was based mainly in the Wynberg area. I was involved in civic organisations as well. That was in the early eighties with Zubeida. We organised the people in Lavender Hill, which is near Muizenberg, into civic and youth formations up to about the mid-eighties or so, when things really started to happen.'

Was your mother ever detained?

'No, she wasn't detained. She was arrested once for being on an illegal march, but was released the same day. They were on a major march in Cape Town, marching for the release of detainees.'

So it sounds like it was instilled in you from quite a young age that as a family you were political.

'We went to school in a place called Diep River. The school was the only so-called coloured institution in the area, which had been declared white. When we went to school on the train, we had to travel in the non-white carriage. That always jarred, but it's funny how these things work. After a while you get used to it and you don't question it.

'Then, of course, you couldn't swim at any of the big beaches in Cape Town, like Muizenberg beach, St James, Kalk Bay. You couldn't go to restaurants there either. Then, when voting took place, that was for only 8–10 per cent of the population. That kind of indignity that you encountered contributed to one's politicisation, ultimately.'

Presumably, a lot of the friends you were going to school with felt the same?

'Not everyone become politicised, and it's amazing to what extent people accept their lot in society. If you look at the history of the world, it's only ever a small minority who take a radical, activist stand and fight the system. The rest of us kind of amble along, going through our lives and seeing that it's wrong, but not doing much about it all. You start accepting a lot of it.

'It's like when slavery ended in the US. Many slaves didn't want to be freed, because they thought their entire destiny was dependent on the power relationship with their master. The psychological aspect is very powerful.'

* * *

Adam Jaffer is Zubeida's much older brother – he is sixty-three to her fifty when we meet at his immaculate house, which is filled with the sounds of birdsong from the aviaries outside and, intermittently, the sound of his dogs barking at passers-by in the street. We sit in the shaded lounge – the scene of many police raids – and talk about what already seems like the distant past, but is still vivid and clear to this soft-spoken man.

'We were just an ordinary family,' Adam says. 'We weren't politically inclined, though we knew we had to stand up against apartheid; we had our principles. But, of course, when Zubeida was detained, that set off a whole chain of events that transformed us into more radical opponents of apartheid. We had a lot of anger towards a system that could have incarcerated her and kept her incognito, and we knew she was tortured. There had already been people murdered in detention; so of course, our fears were great.

128

'Because we were in our twenties, it was our first experience of this nature and we were totally traumatised.' Community, neighbours and family – nobody wanted to get involved; the Jaffers had no support system. That's because people were intimidated by the apartheid behemoth: so many people had been detained – and so many people had died in detention. 'So for us it was very traumatic because we couldn't see Zubeida,' says Adam.

Then she was taken to the Eastern Cape – to separate her from friends and family. But Adam had a plan. 'I used to plant myself outside police stations. Every night I used to go to a different police station and open the bonnet of my car and pretend it was broken. Then, when nobody was looking, I would shout, "Zubeida!" hoping that she was there and she could respond. Of course, nothing happened. I must have gone to about ten or twelve police stations, and there was no response. Every evening I would come back very downhearted, as I couldn't make contact. And then I went to park outside Caledon Square in town, and I actually saw them taking Zubeida to the Eastern Cape.

'We don't like to relive these moments, because it becomes very emotional: to see my little sister being taken between two big burly policemen – it could have been the last time I saw her.'

So you happened to be there.

'I stationed myself there because we had heard she might be taken on that day, and so I don't know if I was lucky or unlucky to see her.'

Did she see you?

'She saw me, yes, and she looked back. I never asked her if she saw me, but she looked like someone who saw me. I waved and I showed the car lights. That's about all I could do.'

Dullah Omar, the family's legal adviser, organised a prison visit for Zubeida's parents a few weeks later, and accompanied them to the Eastern Cape. 'She was in a bad way,' Adam says. 'She told my mother that they were going to kill her, that they had told her they were going to kill her. And so we were in a helpless, hopeless situation.'

By the time Adam himself was detained in 1986, things were

very different. The friends, community and family who were once so intimidated by the regime had become far more militant. There was also support from abroad: money was sent in to cover lawyers' fees, and interdicts would immediately be brought to seek the prisoner's release.

By a bizarre coincidence, Adam was due for an operation on his knee the day Zubeida appeared in court. 'When I woke up from the anaesthetic, the first person I saw was Zubeida, whom I hadn't seen for six weeks. The first place she wanted to come to after her release was the hospital. I thought I was hallucinating. After a few minutes, I realised no, I'm not.'

Zubeida had appeared in court that morning and all charges had been dropped. Spyker van Wyk had tried to have her arrested again, but he had failed.

Her appearance at the hospital is something that Adam will never forget. 'I think that was the most emotional moment of my life. I didn't think I was going to see her alive again.

'Up till today we talk about her ordeal. It has left its mark on all of us, and although we carry on with our lives, that is in our subconscious, and forever it will come back, and one could use the terminology it could haunt you, because that was in the dark days. People who were not involved can talk about these things very lightly, but for us and millions of others who were involved – some to a greater extent, some whose family were killed, murdered or spirited away – I don't think it's so easy just to get over that, you know. It's not very easy.'

Adam's son Reyhaan was terribly affected by his father's incarceration. Adam and his wife Zerene took him to psychologists; he developed a stutter and they had to take him to speech therapists. 'I just disappeared, you see. He was six years old and next minute his dad was gone. How do you explain that to a six-year-old? If you are a criminal, your children can go and visit you; they can say, "There's our dad". But under the detention laws, detention without trial, and especially the State of Emergency of 12 June 1986, the cops were given carte blanche, the rule of law was suspended, and nobody would take responsibility. The security forces and police were given total indemnity from any and all actions.

'Those were dark days. We can talk about it very glibly and lightly today, and when a lot of people talk about it, they say it's the past, it's gone, let's just get on with our lives, but those were the people who were not directly involved, you see. And the people who were directly involved, a lot of them when I meet them today, they are still devastated. Their loved ones have been killed and there is no real support from the state. To think what these people went through...'

And he pauses, this tall, gracious man, as if he is in physical pain. He knows, as the whole family knows, how close they came to losing his youngest sister, their baby, and indeed to losing two of their sons – him and Mansoor.

He pauses and then continues, with effort: 'We were a very close community.' He is now talking about not the Muslim community but the struggle community, the organisations that gave strength to those taken and those left behind. These included the UWCO and the UDF. Through such organisations, political information was disseminated – information that had been effectively withheld for decades from the citizens of South Africa, both black and white (except perhaps for the ruling party and for organisations like the secret, Masonic-style Broederbond[78]).

'Zubeida's detention had a profound effect, not only on us, but on the whole community that we moved in. I think people like Zubeida fired the flame of resistance in the parameters of their own community and their circle of friends.

'So you detain one person, but you inflame 10 000 people. And that's why the State of Emergency of 1986 was the end of the road for the Nationalist Party.' By 1988, some 30 000 people had been arrested.[79] 'Now you quantify that and you times it by 100 or 1 000, and you have made a few million people mad. I think that was the beginning of the end.'

The 1986 State of Emergency was the Nationalist Party's last big crackdown, and it took a terrible toll on people who had begun to hope that their hero Nelson Mandela was about to be released after twenty-seven years' incarceration. From 1986 to 1989 were the hardest three years, Zubeida had confided to me. It seemed the worst thing: to have hope – and to have it cruelly taken away. Then, in February 1990, came the miracle: Mandela came out of prison.

'Most of us, the diehards, even people who were deeply involved with the struggle, didn't know it was going to happen so soon,' says Adam. 'We knew it was the beginning of the end, but we didn't know how much world opinion and economic pressures were bearing on the country – and that the anarchy in South Africa and its ungovernability would lead us to this point. Mandela's release took people by surprise.'

We pause as Reyhaan comes into the room, and Adam does his version of that embarrassing thing all parents do, all around the world. He says: 'He was six years old when I was detained. Look how big he is now.'

I am introduced. 'No, fantastic!' says Reyhaan, grinning and shaking my hand. 'Nice meeting you.' And off he goes, thirty-one years old now, tall and confident.

This was the boy who at just ten years of age went with Adam to see Mandela just after his release. 'I was there at the Grand Parade,' Adam says. 'It was electric, it was just electric, it was a moment not to miss, it was history, it's recorded in your psyche and in your heart. You have witnessed something that you could impart to your children and your grandchildren, tell them about the moment. Fortunately, Reyhaan was a bit older by then and I took him with me, so he also experienced that moment.'[80]

Adam relates the story of their trip down the N2 into town: the mounting excitement, the taxis with the ANC flags, people hanging out of the taxis. 'It was just chaotic, it was something much bigger than the World Cup. When Mandela was released it was something else, the whole country imploded and exploded. People cried – it was very emotional, just to see this man walk out of Victor Verster, when we thought we would never see him alive, we thought we would see him dead, we thought they would carry him out in a box. It was the culmination of many people's struggles and sacrifices that this man was now free. With the kind of resistance we had experienced, we thought the man would never come out. But it happened very, very quickly. History happens very quickly.'

It happened very quickly to Adam too, on one Saturday morning in June 1986, just ahead of the commemoration of the Soweto uprising a decade earlier.

'I had two businesses – a garage and a butcher shop – and I was phoned at the butcher shop to come to the garage because the police were there. They said the police had found some banned stuff at the petrol station, and it was June 16 pamphlets and things like that, nothing dangerous. But then they told me there were about twenty cops there with rifles come to arrest an ordinary guy like me.'

When Adam got to the garage and met the police, he tartly pointed out, 'I'm busy in my business, I'm not running around with hand grenades'. Nevertheless they took him to the police station. 'They said they just wanted to ask me a few questions. But when I got there, one of the security policemen that were also after Zubeida spotted me. And that led to them keeping me there. They first locked me up in the back of a police van because the cells were so full.

'I had nothing to do and I still had my butcher's coat on me. I found a copy of Scope[81] magazine lying in the back of the police van at 1 o'clock on a Saturday. I'm normally running two businesses, but here I am reading Scope [he laughs], and by 1 o'clock I was whisked away to Victor Verster – and I stayed there six weeks.'

His stay included seven days in solitary. But then he was released. He had smuggled a letter out, and Zubeida had brought an interdict that forced the police to take him to court. 'The court found that I was wrongly arrested and detained. If, as the judge asked, I was a dangerous person on 16 June, was I dangerous on 17 June? 16 June had come and gone with no incident, no violence, so what was the reason for detaining me on 17 June? The judge found that they had never applied their minds to the matter – in other words, that they were mindless and they didn't matter,' he jokes, 'and so he freed me.'

The case, *Jaffer v the Minister of Law and Order, 1986*, is in the law books as a precedent. Indeed, in the *Duke Law Magazine* (Summer 1987), there is a reference to the case in an article about apartheid and the South African judiciary:

> Most striking of all has been the judicial response in litigation involving the actions of the police and security forces, under both the permanent security legislation and the states of emergency. Even in strong democracies, such as Britain and the United States, the courts have a predictable tendency to defer to the executive at times of national crisis. Nor should we assume that this occurs only at a time of war; the contrary is amply illustrated by recent cases in both Britain and the United States.
>
> Yet it is in the area of state security that the activism of the South African courts has been greatest. In Natal, the Eastern Cape, the Transvaal and Namibia, in the Appellate Division and in other provincial jurisdictions, judges have rendered ineffective the most broadly phrased unreviewability clauses in the South African statute book. Though expressly forbidden to review the lawfulness of police action in detaining individuals or to grant writs of habeas corpus and related remedies, they have done so repeatedly and have ordered the release of numerous detainees.

How did they treat you in prison?

'The whole system is there to dehumanise you. You sleep on the floor on the cement – no mattress. You go into a bathroom once a day, which is totally filthy, there is slime on the floor, and there's a toilet that's in full view of everybody, so when we were in a communal cell we must sit on the toilet in full view of everyone.

'The whole system is there to break you down. What they didn't realise is that at that stage of the struggle, any such action would only bolster your resolve to fight the system. It made the people more determined, it made them angrier, so what they intended actually worked against it – people would come out of prison and explain what was happening.

'Even the doctors in prison didn't come and see to the hygiene of the ablution blocks, they didn't see to the hygiene of the detainees, so where was the Hippocratic Oath? Just like Steve Biko's death, when those doctors all said, "No, he died of natural causes, he was fit to travel". He was half dead already, but "he was fit to travel", naked in a police van, you know?

'So I think the indictment on the doctors involved for the state was very serious, because the people who came out spoke about these things. The fear was gone now, that fear they had in 1980 was gone. People were practically fearless now, because there were millions of people now involved.'

Zubeida's detention six years earlier had a very different but no less profound effect. It was a watershed event for the Muslim community. She was one of the first Muslims to be detained, and she was certainly the first Muslim woman to be treated so harshly in detention. 'So that also created a lot of inspiration for the Muslim community to wake up and stop banging their heads on the floor, not only having that type of faith, but having the faith to fight injustice and oppression. It swung the whole pendulum in favour of a more radical form of religion, taking up the issues of the community, and the injustice of prejudice and discrimination. It is all mentioned in the holy books: you must fight these things.

'Once you stand up for the poor and the downtrodden, then you have faith with purpose, and that's a big transformation. I think Zubeida played a part in transforming society – in many cases an apathetic, don't-dare society – into a society that started sitting up, and the imams and the Muslim religious leaders started preaching politics, political content, from the pulpit.

'It was probably a first in this country, and so the transformation was tremendous. Zubeida's sacrifice, and the sacrifices of other people like her, weren't in vain, because they radically transformed society. After 1980, the Muslim community was never the same. The Malay ladies who used to only cook and have children were marching in the streets, carrying banners, making food for detainees' families. This was amazing. It didn't happen overnight, but took place because of certain people who made sacrifices.

'And, of course, to about 70 per cent of the community at the time, Zubeida was seen as stupid. "She had a good education," they were saying. "Why does she want to dabble in politics? It's not very Islamic, it's not very religious." We were also damned, you know: they were saying, "What kind of family is this? You must follow the rules of the land and the rulers of the land", and all that. But they didn't add the other part of the sentence: that you follow the rulers of the land if they are just rulers. That's what the books say, not that you should follow blindly.

'But if the rules are unjust and cruel and prejudicial, if they discriminate, then you are obliged not to follow the rules. That's the way it is. So that period of Zubeida's detention, it really woke a lot of people up to the realities of what was really happening. And if you take that period between 1980 and 1985, it's only five years, so brief, and yet the amount of activism in that period was much greater than in 1976, when the Soweto riots started. Then there was a long lull, and from 1980 it then started, and by 1985 it reached a crescendo. And then by 1986 there was a second State of Emergency; that was the beginning of the end.

'A lot must have happened in that five year period to bring about change, not only locally, but internationally also.' There were sanctions, the cultural boycott, the sports boycott. 'These things didn't fall out of the sky; it was the sacrifice of many, many people like Zubeida, and some of them made the ultimate sacrifice.' Like Imam Abdullah Haron, the first Muslim who was killed in detention, and Steve Biko.

136

There was another astonishing thing that happened. The business community put their hands in their pockets and paid for full-page adverts in the *Cape Argus* newspaper carrying the names of all those who had died in detention. That campaign was one of the reasons Adam believes he was detained – that, and his connection to Zubeida. But more importantly, he says, the fact that businesses would finance the adverts showed the transformation in attitude among the population generally. 'Prior to 1980 the business people wouldn't touch you,' he explains. 'If you asked for a contribution, they would say, "I don't want to get involved".'

What was significant to Adam was that when he was detained, he was interrogated three times by the security police, and the thrust of their questioning was, how could the Muslim community turn from a very passive to a very radical community? 'They wanted to know, "Who's behind it? Who's spurring them on? Who's instigating?" And I had to explain to them that nobody is instigating people, this is the way they feel. This is spontaneous.'

There had been the incident in Salt River in 1985 that Mansoor had mentioned, where the police went into a home and killed the owner, Ebrahim Carelse. The funeral was held the following day, as is customary in the Muslim faith. It was attended by some 30 000 people. 'I happened to be one of the marshals,' Adam recalls. 'Right at the head of the funeral as we moved up Salt River to the cemetery, there were two cops standing there for some reason – for some mad reason, because you don't confront a crowd of 30 000. One cop ran away – the other one was confrontational, because he took out his gun and got into an altercation, and a shot went off.' He had shot an elderly man in the stomach. 'Then the crowd just went wild and tore this cop to pieces.'

Dr Farid Esack, an academic who has served as a Commissioner for Gender Equality in South Africa, tried to intervene, but some of the mob pulled him off and kicked the policeman senseless. 'Then they took a pavement slab and they dropped it on his head.'

137

The policeman was just twenty-three, a coloured man but one who looked white, as he was very fair, says Adam. It was possibly a factor that might have influenced the angry crowd – who knows?

'The white establishment was very shocked at what happened, because this very placid, very quiet Muslim community had now become so radical that they murdered a policeman, a known policeman, without blinking an eye. Such was the anger that was building up.'

Two men – Gassan Solomons, who died recently, and Sheikh Gabier – made radical political statements from the podium at Carelse's funeral. They were forced into exile as they were being sought by the police, who blamed them for inflaming the crowd and causing the death of the policeman. But it was the policeman who inflamed the crowd, Adam points out. 'If he wasn't there, nothing would have happened. But the police felt so powerful that one cop could stand in front of 30 000 and you can't touch him, because he was a cop. But the mood had changed. This was a watershed event in the history of the Muslim community, when they made it clear they would not allow their members to be killed or detained and murdered in detention without taking action.

'That was very significant, too, in that we also felt a bit safer. Because if we got detained by the police, there would be that restraint – the Muslim community would march in their thousands to the prison.'

At the time, Zubeida and her then husband Johnny Issel were on the run. That led to a raid on Adam's house. 'About twenty cops with guns came to look for her. No search warrants, nothing.' Adam wouldn't let them in until they handed over their ID; then he made them wait until he got dressed. 'I speak good Afrikaans,' he said. 'They got a bit of a shock, because I was speaking to them in their language, you see. When they came in, there were a few uniformed policewomen with them and they said, "O, *meneer, jy het 'n mooi huis* [You've got a nice house]". I said, "Yes, we're not terrorists, we live like this! We are normal people, we live normal lives. What are you people doing here?"

138

'Being politically minded does not make you a terrorist. If you stand up for your principles, it doesn't mean you are a terrorist. In a way, the police were indoctrinated, you see.'

This terrible system was so successful, so effective in dividing everyone completely.

'It was 100 per cent successful. The systems of apartheid are still very much in place today. I am still living on this side of the railway line and the whites are still living on the other side of the line. After fifteen years of democracy, it's economic apartheid.

'You can't afford to live in those areas. I was born in Parow, in the heart of Afrikanerdom. We were thrown out of there, then we moved to Maitland and we were thrown out of there, and then we moved to Claremont and we were thrown out of there. But now we can't afford to move back into Claremont, because they want three million rand for the house now. It's economic apartheid. The apartheid system was very successful.'

I went to an equestrian event on Sunday with a friend I was staying with. It was out at Wellington on a big wine farm; the wealth was immense. We saw one black rider, but everyone else was white. There were massive four-by-fours and huge horseboxes and glossy horses, which would have cost a fortune, and all the white mothers and daughters with their horses ... I thought, Well, what has changed?

'Fundamentally, very little has changed. What BEE [the Black Economic Empowerment policy] has done is made some people rich and the rest have just stayed behind. So black economic empowerment has not been successful; it has been confined to a few. And, of course, our Constitution is not applicable to all the people. We don't have security, we don't have healthcare, we don't have schooling, we don't have housing, we don't have jobs. We must live behind barbed-wire fences and electric fences, with dogs and guns.

'There is 45 per cent unemployment. There are 18 000 murders a year, 100 000 rapes a year, besides those that are not reported. Our HIV rate is the highest in the world, the divorce rate is 50 per cent. We hold the record for just about everything. And the gap between the rich and the poor in South Africa is the largest: we've now beaten Brazil for the disparity between rich and poor.[82]

'So one in two marriages fail. That is the highest rate in the world, and it's simply because of the economic situation – high unemployment, high crime. What we must question is, have we progressed?

'If you ask the average person, they will say that they were better off under apartheid. Because we are now in a kind of anarchy. Of those 18 000 murderers, only 10 per cent are ever apprehended. And of that 10 per cent, only 10 per cent are ever prosecuted. So we are talking a total of 1 per cent of murderers being brought to trial.'

Your detention must have been a big shock to Zerene.

'She was left with two businesses to run and my son to see to, and she is just an ordinary, placid person. It transformed her life, because suddenly she was thrust into this.'

Did that experience make her political too?

'It did make her political, because she then took very serious chances.' He tells the story of Zerene, the lift and the letter, which his mother had already shared with me. 'And that must have been very worrying for her, because if they had caught her they would have arrested her. So she turned from a very quiet, passive person to a person who would do a thing like that.'

Your whole family has been really touched by this.

'There's a lot of anger in us for what they did to Zubeida. And that anger transformed into action, and it actually inspired us in a very perverted way. You don't want that kind of inspiration really.'

Another inspiration was Guy. 'He inspired Zubeida and all of us because of the stand he took, and the suffering he went through.'

The system brutalised the white interrogators too, Adam points out. 'They are committing suicide; they are in insane institutions; they are alcoholics, drug addicts. You see, this system secretly brutalised them also. How must they feel now that they realise that what they were doing was wrong? When you brutalise someone, you are doing

140

harm to yourself also.'

He says of Frans Mostert, who tortured Zubeida: 'Maybe he is sickly, maybe he has become more churchly now, maybe he wants to reconcile what he did in the past. If you are religious, then you've got to answer one day.'

The post-apartheid era has brought different issues. 'This is a different struggle for a different era and for different reasons. We succeeded in overcoming apartheid: it is a victory. But what is happening now is that the poor are not being uplifted, and that is very sad because it was a part of our struggle to uplift the poor. And the poor are being exploited more with globalisation, contract working and casual working. How can you run your life if you work only one day a week?'

* * *

I make my farewells and drive back down to the sea. I'm not far from the area where poor Anni Dewani was driven before being murdered: Harare, not far from Muizenberg and bordering the great sprawl of Khayelitsha. I need to get to the supermarket – Barbara has asked friends over for supper tonight, and it's my turn to cook. And in a quick half-hour my trolley will be filled with more food than any Harare resident could afford in a month. South Africa is the same infuriating land of privilege and poverty, natural beauty and the ugliness of deprivation, abuse and violence against women.

Yet in 2009, when I had driven into Khayelitsha with another friend from my year at Rhodes, David Bristow, we had seen brand-new houses with solar panels, rows of portable toilets, thriving businesses in shipping containers, two-lane paved roads as well as dirt tracks. We had met two young men eager to talk about their allegiance to COPE, the political party newly formed to fight the election.

The next day I am on the road to Hermanus. I had come to South Africa to research this book, but I was also there to see my mother, who was beginning to slip away from us. On weekends I would drive out to my parents' retirement complex in the old black BMW my mother no longer used, and she and I would go out for tea somewhere along the coast. My father, then eighty-five years old but continuing to work as a publisher, was still able to make regular trips to the UK, but my mother could no longer travel. Losing her would be a heartbreak I wasn't ready to face.

Sometimes she would be animated and talkative; at other times she was quiet. Woven into this trip to Hermanus is the quiet dread I feel each time I drive out to see her. How will she be? I am thinking about my three interviewees; their families have played a huge part in their stories, the parents not always understanding what their children were doing, but always showing love and support.

That is just how my mother has always been: whatever my sister and I did, we were the best, the most beautiful and the most precious, as were her grandchildren. She never forgot a birthday or a single fact about our lives; an important interview or exam would find her praying for us. She stood up for me when as a teenager I went out with a long-haired, motorbike-riding boy my father didn't approve of; she saw quite clearly that he was a gentle soul. Her dancer's body was only a scant five feet four inches, yet she would shoo me out of the door on a date and tell me, 'Don't worry – I'll deal with your father'.

She wasn't like other mothers. She was as stylish and beautiful as they were, yes, but she didn't write menus; she worked. And she loved the arts fiercely. She and I went to Cape Town's only arts cinema to see Bergman, Pinter and Chabrol. Ignoring the whites-only Nico Malan (now the Artscape Theatre Centre) with its safe Ayckbourn, Stoppard and Simon Gray, we went to the Space Theatre run by Brian Astbury and Yvonne Bryceland, who had neatly sidestepped apartheid law on mixed-race audiences by creating a members' club. We saw Athol Fugard with Bryceland in his own *Boesman en Lena*, as well as plays by Tennessee Williams and John Osborne and movies by John Ford. She loved ballet the best of all. Yet all that was gone now.

My trip was almost over; the last weekend with my mother had come too soon. And then it snowed in England, so heavily that my taxi driver phoned me and said he couldn't fetch me from Heathrow, because he couldn't get out of the driveway. So I got to stay in South Africa a few more days.

My mother and I continued to go on our drives. Now and then we might stop to catch a glimpse of the whales in the bay, and I would see her face light up in excitement. On the last morning, we drove to the gate of her complex, and just as I was reflecting on how much she must live in the moment and how little she could remember of the day before, she said, 'Let's *not* go to Duchies today'. She waved her hand, indicating we should go further. 'Let's go down to Onrus. Dad and I always used to go down there. And we used to walk along the seafront. I really liked that.'

Onrus was home to their favourite restaurant of old. Overlooking the green lagoon and the beach, it was run by Frank, who always came by to chat. We had coffee and muffins. Frank came over to say hello.

Then we walked along the seafront and sat on the bench. 'Just look at that seagull,' she said. 'When I come back, I want to be a seagull.' And she let her head fall back to watch its swooping flight.

We sat for a while longer. She pointed to the waves. 'Just look at that,' she said. 'They're saying, "What *more* do you need?" '

So then, that was why I came to South Africa, I thought, holding her hand tight. It wasn't to write a book on the survivors of the brutal system of apartheid. It was to do this. To sit on the seafront and look at the waves and hold my mother's hand. Before it was too late.

Sussex

It is 16 December 2013, Reconciliation Day, and a day many have been dreading: the day after Nelson Mandela's funeral, the day when we are all to ask, What happens now?

I contact Marion in South Africa and I ask her what she thinks his legacy is. I ask her what she thinks his legacy is. 'How does one begin to describe the legacy of Nelson Mandela?' she answers. 'Steve Biko said that "in time we shall be able to bestow upon South Africa the greatest possible gift – a more human face". And that is what Madiba has done, not just for South Africa but for the entire world.'

And what are her memories of Mandela? 'Janice, I'm afraid I simply won't have the time to share all the personal memories now. I met him for the first time when he visited us in Pretoria Central Prison after his release from Robben Island. And I was privileged enough to get know him and work with him at Shell House[83] from 1991 to 1994, when I worked with Cyril Ramaphosa in the secretary general's office. I also knew him, of course, as a member of the National Executive Committee. I had a very close connection with him, as I think did most people who worked with him – not just as a leader, but also as a father and a friend when that was needed.'

I manage to reach Zubeida on the phone the night before she leaves for a Christmas holiday with friends in Rwanda. That morning I had seen the heartfelt open letter to the *Washington Post* she wrote in response to an article by the US journalist Anne Applebaum.

Applebaum had written:

> In Johannesburg a few months ago, I asked a young, black and politically savvy South African journalist how his newspaper would cover Nelson Mandela's death. He shook his head: He dearly wished not to have to cover it at all. 'I just hope I'm not in the office that day. I just hope I'm away, maybe in a different country.'
>
> He knew, of course, what Mandela's death would bring: a moment of national reckoning, an assessment of 'what have we achieved' in the years since Mandela's release from prison in 1990 and his inauguration as South Africa's first black president in 1994. I told him that what was written in the wake of Mandela's death would probably reveal less about the man and more about his country. He agreed: That's exactly what he didn't want to have to face.

Zubeida's response is tart and to the point: she is coldly critical of Applebaum's journalism – taking a response from one black journalist and turning it into a trend, as if she has taken the temperature of the nation by speaking to one man.[84]

> Your opinion piece last week was so predictable – an old tired narrative: as soon as Mandela goes, his party will implode and his country will go to the dogs. Thirty years ago, the narrative was: as soon as Mandela comes out of prison, his party will drive the whites into the sea and his country will go to the dogs. It is a narrative that is strongest amongst those who base their analyses and interpretations on fear and not on hope, on opinion not fact ... there seems to be a tendency among the international media to separate the man from his political home and to honour him and rubbish his home. It is a strange phenomenon.
>
> Why do you repeat a predictable narrative that chooses to celebrate our decline rather than our progress? You visited South Africa and spoke with a young journalist and decided that his view was representative of all our views. I too can write about your country and point out

145

that your official figures state that over 11 million people are presently unemployed. The unofficial figures stand at 17 million.

I too can conclude that your democracy is in trouble because for a long while now under 40 per cent of your people have voted in each election. It was only in the last election when President Barack Obama brought some hope that you could push that up to 53.6 per cent. Let's not talk about the 10,717 gun deaths this year alone or the 188,380 victims of sexual assault recorded by your Justice Department in 2010. I too can string together facts and paint a lopsided picture of your country.

We had arranged to speak by telephone. I want to know her reaction to Mandela's death and the aftermath, what she thinks is coming. What is the outlook now for South Africa?

We haven't got much time to talk – she has to pack. But she is more upbeat-sounding than I have heard her be for a long time. She tells me that one of her most powerful memories will be seeing people filing past Madiba's body lying in state in the Union Buildings. 'There are images that will remain in my mind. People broke down in tears as they passed the body. I saw a woman in military uniform, with blonde hair, putting her arm around a black citizen. We are used to associating the military with punishment and cruelty – to see that was enough to make me cry. I know there are challenges and there is still a lot to be done, but to see this ...'

Unlike many of those who filed past Madiba's body, Zubeida has a sense of loss that comes from a long personal association with Mandela. First, when he was on Robben Island and she had been arrested and tortured the first time, he smuggled out a message of support to her. Those on the island had seen the articles she had written, he said, which were giving them 'a lot of hope', but they were concerned about what was happening to her. When he was released in 1990, she joined in the celebrations at the Bishopscourt house of Desmond Tutu, then archbishop of Cape Town. Zubeida says of that event, 'Walter Sisulu

SUSSEX

came up to me and said that they had followed my life from the island.'

Mandela himself was warm and supportive. When funds for her bursary for an MA at the University of Columbia in New York seemed in doubt, Mandela stepped in. 'He raised all the money,' says Zubeida. 'It was instantly sorted.'

However, they did part ways a decade later over a statement Mandela made following the 9/11 destruction of the World Trade Center in New York. He was at the White House with then president George W. Bush, who declared his intention of bombing Iraq and Osama bin Laden. Mandela released a statement that was similar in tone, seeming to approve of Bush's position. There was an outcry, and Zubeida, among others, wrote a piece published in the *Independent* expressing her difference of opinion.

Once back in South Africa, he sent a message to Zubeida inviting her to come to breakfast with him. 'I couldn't go because I was fasting,' she says.

Two weeks later she was invited again, but this time she was travelling. Then, five months later, Raghmat Jaffer went up to Mandela at a gathering. 'Your daughter doesn't want to meet with me,' he said. 'Tell her to come and see me.' By then, says Zubeida, he had changed his statement in reaction to the response.

The next day, Zubeida went to see him in his house in Bishopscourt, and Mandela went through his statement line by line, justifying why he had said what he had said. But Zubeida says she was hardly listening. 'It was Valentine's Day, and I was so overwhelmed by seeing him sitting against the window with the flowers in the garden behind him and the mountain beyond that. It was just so amazing.'

And now, more than a decade later, she struggled with her emotions while watching the crowds at the Union Building. 'I had seen him walk up the steps and speak there, and now he was in his coffin. But I also thought of the journey we had made in twenty years. At the inauguration it was tense: De Klerk was tense, his wife was very tense. You can see it if you look at the pictures. But if you look at these ten

147

days at the Union Buildings, the military in charge were quite relaxed and noticeably affected, black and white. We had come so far. I was proud it was open to everybody. People filed past in their thousands.

'Then going through to Qunu and the rural areas, seeing the simplicity of the life and being aware of where he came from – where he started off and where he got to. Lots of young people feel they can do anything and get their education because of what Madiba did. The whole experience has been really affirming.'

However, some of the journalistic response was out of kilter with the reality of the country, she says. 'We as journalists have to ask ourselves deep questions – we have to reflect what is going on. We are not here to be cynical and disparaging. I think for me it raises a lot of questions about our journalism and our attitudes. Most journalists have been upbeat, showing what is happening around the country, but when I read the *Washington Post* piece – I'm so tired of the old refrain that we are all going to the dogs; that is so *not* understanding the complexity of our situation.

'The funeral, though, was such a perfect ending. It also showcased the quality leaders we have on the continent. It is unfair on the nations around the world not to be given proper information about Africa. We will always have dramas, but everything is not breaking apart.'

What are the challenges that lie ahead? Job creation lies at the top of the list. 'It's probably the biggest challenge,' Zubeida says. 'The crime statistics have gone down every year, little by little. They are still not acceptable. We do have a lot of violence, but it's just a matter of time.'

And as we wrap up – she still has to pack for her holiday in an African country whose own history has been marked by terrible bloodshed – she adds: 'We are in for the long haul; our families are here. We are not going anywhere else. We have got to work to make this as good as possible.'

We say goodbye and I wish her well until we meet again – perhaps next year, at the fourth democratic elections. It will be twenty years since democracy flowered in this land of ours: a cause for celebration.

There will be just one reason for me to mourn. My mother has been dead for two years, and on the headland at Westcliffe, where we scattered her ashes into the bright sea, stands a bench with her name on it.

The morning after, I had taken a kayak out into Walker Bay, and as we stroked our way up the coast to that spot below the cliffs, I found I had as companion a young Afrikaner with a philosopher's mind, who said two things that comforted me. *Death is just the beginning of the biggest adventure,* he told me. I hoped he was right: I could not believe that her spirit had gone forever. We shipped our paddles and floated at the spot where the ashes had fallen, and he said that in the winter, he and his companions, battling the winds up this coast, would often pull into the shelter of this headland. He would think of her when he next turned his kayak in there, he said.

We headed out to sea. There were still whales in the bay, and I wished fervently that a shape as large as my grief would rise from the depths and fix us with a basilisk eye.

We turned. The coast was a nothing but a slim shelf on the horizon; the tourmaline sea rippled and sang about us. Yet this, I thought, was the extraordinary and limitless country in which the satirical cartoonist Zapiro had told me of being at a meeting where Julius Malema had called for his death – and no-one had demurred; that he had been sued for millions by President Jacob Zuma – and had had further death threats – yet he was still alive. A country in which the investigative magazine *Noseweek* had thrived through countless lawsuits, once re-vived by generous readers to publish again, whose editor Martin Welz told me he fears nothing and nobody.

A country where my best friend from childhood, the botanist Fiona Powrie, had a flat tyre by the side of the N2 to Paarl late at night. As she stood nervously beside her truck with a tyre iron in her hand, the man who approached said, 'Can I change that for you?' He had been guarding the nearby roadworks.'Write *that* down,' she told me.

This was the country in which my mother had lived from the mid-twenties for nearly ninety years, and had seen it swerve from the milder rule of Smuts, when there was thought of eventual black en-franchisement, to Nationalist control after the Second World War (in which her brothers had flown for the RAF, while many Afrikaners had joined the Brownshirts), through the years of comfortable wealth for whites against desperate poverty for blacks, through the Sharpeville massacre, the Soweto uprising, Mandela's release, the Boipateng mas-sacre, the first democratic vote and Mandela as President.

She was there for the gradual disenchantment with the presidents who followed Mandela, and yes, throughout, was living in a country of kindness, desperation, sacrifice, contradiction and, ultimately, freedom.

This is the country where, every day, people are seeing what needs to be done and doing it, where the imperfections of government are countered by the actions of ordinary citizens.

Where a girl called Ruschka, who had narrowly escaped being poi-soned in her mother's womb, had grown up free to cast her first vote – the daughter of a liberation hero.

It was her country. My country. It belonged to all of us. It would flow onward, from mother to daughter, onward and upward. And thanks to those who had laid their lives on the line, it had a future.

'We need to go back now,' I said to the young man, and we turned the kayak.

Acknowledgements

FIRST, OF COURSE, MY UNDYING THANKS go to Zubeida, Marion and Guy, who so open-heartedly shared their story with me. And there are a host of others who came forward, advised, talked to me and, in some cases, had me to stay and fed me: Jeanne Berger, Mrs Raghmat Jaffer, Adam and Mansoor Jaffer, Tony Pinchuck, Devan Pillay, Les Switzer, Rob Harrewyn, Rory and Lynn Macnamara. Thanks also to Barbara McCrea and Gabriel Pinchuck for having me to stay (and Gabriel for giving up his room for me and moving into a smaller one); to Maggie Davey and Bridget Impey for having the courage and generosity of spirit not only to publish this book, but to hold on tight through three years of crisis until the manuscript was delivered; to Lisa Compton for being a meticulous and sympathetic editor; and to Lara Jacob and Kerrie Barlow for their skill and patience in seeing the project through. Thanks to Ruth Sunderland for her encouragement, John Mulholland of *The Observer* for his interest in the original article and Allan Jenkins of the *Observer* Magazine for his patience and excellent advice on its structure. I thank my son and daughter, Dominic and Imogen Warman Roup, for as ever being unfalteringly loving and encouraging; Julian Roup for keeping calm and making me delicious food through three years of after-work and weekend writing; my father, George Warman, for his enthusiasm and advice; my beloved mother, Lynne Warman, whom we lost almost two years ago now; and Herman and Teri Roup for a life-saving holiday in Santa Barbara halfway through. And for everything else: Fiona Powrie. Jeanne Samuels. Liz Wildi. Fiona Archer. Gail Walker. Friends and sisters: they are the best.

Janice Warman
East Sussex
1 May 2014

Endnotes

1 Antjie Krog, *Country of My Skull* (London: Jonathan Cape, 1998), pp. 184–185.
2 Peter Bruce was Wendy Woods's brother.
3 The Progressive Federal Party (PFP), successor to the Progressive Party, was formed in 1977, after a group of liberal members of the United Party (UP) broke away to form a parliamentary opposition against apartheid.
4 Ronnie Kasrils served as the former head of intelligence for the military wing of the ANC. He was a member of the Central Committee of the South African Communist Party, a member of the ANC National Executive Committee, and minister of intelligence services from 2004 to 2008.
5 Joe Slovo (1926–1995) was a prominent anti-apartheid activist, a long-time leader of the South African Communist Party, a leading member of the ANC and a commander of the ANC's military wing. He served as minister of housing under Nelson Mandela.
6 Afrikaans for 'slippery jackal'.
7 The ANC was based in Lusaka for the majority of years in exile (1963–1994).
8 The Soweto uprising began when more than 20 000 school pupils marched to protest against the use of Afrikaans as a medium of instruction in black secondary schools. It escalated into a nationwide revolt, sparking the next wave of the struggle for liberation.
9 Ingrid Jonker was a prominent South African poet (1933–1965).
10 Republic Day, 31 May, was a public holiday in South Africa during the apartheid years, celebrating the withdrawal of the country from the British Commonwealth. It was discontinued in 1994 after the first democratic elections.
11 Bophuthatswana was a designated black 'homeland' under the apartheid government. Part of the territory lay close to the Botswana border.

12 Peter Richer later became deputy director general of the National Intelligence Agency for the post-apartheid government.

13 Ruth First was murdered in August 1982 by a parcel bomb in Maseru, Lesotho. See http://en.wikipedia.org/wiki/Ruth_First.

14 The MPLA, or the People's Movement for the Liberation of Angola, is the political party that has ruled Angola since the country won independence from Portugal in 1975.

15 SWAPO, the South West African People's Organisation, began as a liberation movement advocating the independence of Namibia (formerly South West Africa) from South African rule; it is now Namibia's ruling party.

16 Martin Thembisile 'Chris' Hani was chief of staff of Umkhonto we Sizwe and general secretary of the South African Communist Party. He was assassinated in 1993 by Janusz Waluś, an anti-Communist refugee with close links to the white supremacist group AWB.

17 Norman Manoim was an anti-apartheid lawyer; he has served as chairperson of the Competition Tribunal since 2009.

18 Anti-apartheid lawyer Peter Harris is the author of *In a Different Time: The Inside Story of the Delmas Four* (Cape Town: Umuzi, 2008), the account of four captured ANC cadres who were sentenced to death after refusing to plead guilty at their trial, insisting they were essentially prisoners of war and so did not recognise the court as legitimate.

19 Robert McBride was a member of Umkhonto we Sizwe during the apartheid years. Three people died and sixty-nine others were injured in the bombing of Magoo's Bar in Durban on 14 June 1986. McBride led the MK cell who laid the bomb, believing the bar was frequented by security police. He was sentenced to death, but later released.

20 South African commandos killed thirty ANC activists and twelve Lesotho nationals in a cross-border raid on Maseru on 9 December 1982.

21 DraftFCB Social Marketing won its first Loerie Award in the *ubuntu* category last year and was selected by the World Economic Forum from hundreds of submissions from across the globe to be part of the launch of its Creative for Good website at the Cannes International Festival of Creativity.

22 The Homecoming Revolution is an initiative set up in 2003 to encourage South Africans living abroad to return to their home country.

23 The riots were caused by serious social and economic problems affecting Britain's inner cities, said the Scarman Report the following year, which blamed 'racial disadvantage that is a fact of British life'.

24 The 1985 All Blacks tour to South Africa was cancelled after legal action

on the grounds that it would breach the New Zealand Rugby Union's constitution. It was part of the general sporting boycott of South Africa during apartheid, which had begun with the 1964 Summer Olympics when the International Olympics Committee withdrew its invitation on discovering the country's teams would not be racially integrated.

25 The United Party was South Africa's ruling party between 1934 and 1948, when the National Party took power. It then became the main opposition party until the Progressive Federal Party broke away and formed a new opposition.

26 On 21 March 1960, sixty-nine black people were shot and killed by police and 180 others were injured during a demonstration against the pass laws held outside the municipal offices in Sharpeville.

27 *Ubuntu* can be translated as 'humanness'; it has come to mean 'humanity towards others', but also implies the deep understanding of the universal bond that connects humanity. The word has been more recently popularised, because of its use by Nelson Mandela, Desmond Tutu and others.

28 Dr Ivan Toms was Cape Town's director of health, at one time the sole doctor servicing a population of 60 000 at the Crossroads squatter camp outside Cape Town. He was persecuted by the apartheid regime for his homosexuality (then a criminal offence) and for his role as founder and leader of the End Conscription Campaign. He was sentenced to twenty-one months in prison for refusing call-up to a military camp.

29 *Mail and Guardian*, 25 August 2008.

30 The National Party is the ruling party that created and ran the system of apartheid from 1948 to 1990.

31 The pass laws required all black people to carry reference books with their personal details (including their names, tax codes and employer details). Anyone found in public without a pass book could be detained for up to thirty days.

32 Balthazar Johannes ('B.J.' or 'John') Vorster was the NP prime minister from 1966 to 1978 and president from 1978 to 1979.

33 The PAC is a Black Africanist movement founded by Robert Sobukwe in April 1959, when a number of members broke away from the ANC; it is now a political party.

34 The stayaway was called in October 1976 as a solidarity gesture with those killed in the Soweto uprising three months earlier. There was a very active Black Consciousness Movement in the Grahamstown townships. Notwithstanding its focus on black pride, it was prepared to co-operate – on its terms – with white student sympathisers. The handful of Rhodes

students involved had helped with preparation and distribution of pamphlets for the work stayaway, but only the black activists were convicted and sentenced.

35 'Banned' people were confined to their homes and not allowed to see more than one person at a time. They could not be quoted.

36 The *Voice* was a weekly newspaper with a Christian and Black Consciousness orientation, which also covered anti-apartheid issues. The *World* and *Weekend World* took an anti-apartheid stance under their editor in chief Percy Qoboza, who was detained twice, the second time for six months, before leaving South Africa. The papers were banned and members of the editorial staff detained in 1977. In the late seventies, six of the staff disappeared. The *World* photographer Sam Nzima took the iconic photograph of Hector Pieterson in the Soweto uprising on 16 June 1976.

37 Evidence to the Truth and Reconciliation Commission, 3 March 1999; see http://www.justice.gov.za/trc/media%5C1999%5C9903/s990303a.htm.

38 *The Independent*, 13 February 1999.

39 *Mail and Guardian*, 29 May 2008.

40 Masazane was a project of the South African Institute of Race Relations in East London, aimed at promoting political dialogue and friendships across racial divisions.

41 In 1968 the apartheid government set up the South African Indian Council, supposedly to represent the interests of the Indian population, but it was widely rejected. By 1974 half of the members were elected; in 1981 the election was boycotted.

42 The late president Nelson Mandela gave a speech from the dock at the Rivonia Trial in 1964 that convicted him and seven comrades to twenty-seven years imprisonment. It went down in history for its power but particularly for its conclusion, which reverberated around the world: 'During my lifetime, I have dedicated my life to this struggle of the African people. I have fought against white domination, and I have fought against black domination. I have cherished the ideal of a democratic and free society in which all persons will live together in harmony and with equal opportunities. It is an ideal for which I hope to live for and to see realised. But, my Lord, if it needs be, it is an ideal for which I am prepared to die.'

43 Robben Island, which lies in Table Bay off Cape Town, is well known for the fact that Nelson Mandela was imprisoned there for eighteen of the twenty-seven years he spent in prison. He was one of many political prisoners held there, including Mac Maharaj, the poet Dennis Brutus, Jacob Zuma, Govan Mbeki, Walter Sisulu and Tokyo Sexwale.

44 The Group Areas Act, passed in 1950, enforced the segregation of the different races to separate geographical areas; it also restricted ownership and occupation of land.

45 The UDF, which was launched in 1983 in Mitchells Plain, Cape Town, was an anti-apartheid body that incorporated many anti-apartheid organisations. Its formation was the result of social, economic and political changes since the Soweto uprising in 1976.

46 Oupa Monareng is a South African politician, a former ANC member and a member of the National Assembly (2004–2009); he served on the Johannesburg Mayoral Committee with the portfolio for economic development.

47 The literal translation of the Afrikaans word *kak* is 'shit'; here it means 'suffer'.

48 Delta was a student club formed in response to the government's mass resettlement of people at Thornhill, with the aim of assisting these refugees from the government's policy of making the Transkei region into an 'independent' Bantustan. The club had some twenty members who went to Thornhill resettlement camp to help with community development projects.

49 In the late 1970s four young men refused South Africa's compulsory call-up. The movement grew and in 1983 the End Conscription Campaign was formed. The Committee on South African War Resistance (COSAWR) was founded by political exiles in London and Amsterdam in the late seventies.

50 The IDAF was formed to help those escaping conscription in South Africa during the apartheid years.

51 Thornhill was one of the resettlement camps created in the Eastern Cape by the apartheid government's forced removals policy of the late 1970s.

52 A non-violent white women's resistance organisation formed in South Africa by Jean Sinclair.

53 Walter Sisulu was an anti-apartheid activist and former secretary general and deputy president of the ANC, who was imprisoned for twenty-five years on Robben Island.

54 *The Guardian*, 18 February 2013.

55 Reconstruction and Development Programme houses. The RDP was instituted by the government of Nelson Mandela in 1994 to address the socio-economic problems caused by the lengthy struggle against apartheid.

56 At Nelson Mandela's memorial service, the sign-language interpreter's gestures were meaningless. Thamsanqa Jantjie, a qualified interpreter, said he had suffered 'an attack of schizophrenia'.

57 South Africa's ombudsman, Public Protector Thuli Madsonela, ruled that Zuma had spent public money on an upgrade to his property at Nkandla, including a visitors' lounge, amphitheatre, cattle enclosure, swimming pool and houses for the president's relatives. However, just before the 2014 election, a committee set up to investigate Nkandla was dissolved.

58 Julius Malema is leader of the Economic Freedom Fighters, a political movement founded in 2013, and former president of the ANC Youth League. He was expelled from the ANC in 2012.

59 Jonathan Shapiro (Zapiro) is a satirical cartoonist famous for lampooning the government and, in particular, for portraying President Jacob Zuma with a shower attached to his head, referring to Zuma's acquittal for rape of a young female relative who was HIV-positive. Zuma said he had showered following sex to protect himself from infection.

60 *The Spear* depicts President Jacob Zuma with his genitals exposed and forms part of artist Brett Murray's *Hail to the Thief II* exhibition. The artwork caused a national outcry and was labelled racist by the ANC.

61 The South African Broadcasting Corporation was a government-controlled state monopoly under apartheid.

62 J. Edgar Hoover was director of the US Federal Bureau of Investigation (FBI) for forty-eight years until his death in 1972. He became known for using the organisation to intimidate political dissenters and activists, and to collect evidence using illegal methods.

63 An anti-Islamic video that sparked rioting in Egypt and elsewhere. Portrayed as a trailer for a full-length film to be shown in the West, it shows Christians being attacked and a medical clinic trashed by a Muslim mob in Egypt, followed by a retelling of the story of Muhammad, which has been overdubbed with Islamophobic lines.

64 Leaks from Edward Snowden revealed the US National Security Agency's mass surveillance of its own citizens. The revelations were broken in *The Guardian*. Further reports in *The Guardian* and the *Washington Post* have led to a White House review into data surveillance and the introduction of a number of congressional reform bills.

65 There are 144 reported rapes in South Africa each day, but research on under-reporting shows that the real figure could be as high as 3 600 rapes per day. 'Up to 3,600 Rapes in SA Every Day', *IOL News*, 8 February 2013, www.iol.co.za/news/crime-courts/up-to-3-600-rapes-in-sa-every-day-1.1466429#.Uva1End_sfk.

66 Formed as a result of parents' reactions to the 1976 uprisings, UWCO aimed to unite women against apartheid.

67 'Spyker' van Wyk was a notorious torturer under apartheid. According to the Truth and Reconciliation Final Report (Volume 3, Chapter 5, subsection 8): 'In the evidence before the Commission, Warrant Officer Hernus JP "Spyker" van Wyk is the individual most consistently associated with torture in the Western Cape over a thirty year period.'

68 Frans Mostert was another notorious apartheid torturer. Eventually he met Zubeida's ex-husband, the activist Johnny Issel, whom he had also tortured, at Issel's request. As stated in the Truth and Reconciliation Commission Final Report (Volume 3, Chapter 5): 'Captain Frans Mostert became known for his methods of intimidation, assault, and particularly sexual threats directed at female detainees'.

69 The *Cape Times* ran Zubeida's in-depth investigation into the shootings during rioting on the Cape Flats, during which at least forty-two people were killed. See Zubeida's Press Freedom Address at Rhodes University (1996) on her website: http://www.zubeidajaffer.co.za/articles/46-annual-press-freedom-address.html.]

70 Quoted in Zubeida Jaffer, *Our Generation* (Cape Town: Kwela, 2003), pp. 184–185.

71 Antjie Krog, *Country of My Skull* (London: Jonathan Cape, 1998), p. 185.

72 Jaffer, *Our Generation* (Cape Town: Kwela, 2003), p. 21.

73 Jaffer, *Our Generation*, p. 21.

74 Jaffer, *Our Generation*, p. 26.

75 Jaffer, *Our Generation*, pp. 31–33.

76 Jaffer, *Our Generation*, p. 69

77 The word *saamstan* is Afrikaans for 'stand together'. The story of the *Saamstan* newspaper is now the subject of a documentary film titled, *Saamstan Again*.

78 The Broederbond was a secret, men-only, Afrikaner Calvinist organisation in South Africa often compared to the Freemasons.

79 Brian McKendrick and Wilma Hoffmann, *People and Violence in South Africa* (Cape Town: Oxford University Press, 1990), p. 62.

80 After his release in 1990, Nelson Mandela gave his first speech at Cape Town's Grand Parade to a crowd of 150 000–250 000 who had waited for five hours to see him.

81 *Scope* was a popular men's magazine.

82 These figures are for 2010.

83 Shell House, now known as Luthuli House, is the headquarters of the ANC.

84 See http://bookslive.co.za/blog/2013/12/11/zubeida-jaffer-responds-to-washington-post-op-ed-by-anne-applebaum-on-nelson-mandelas-death/.